PRE-ABRAHAMIC PROPHETS –
NOOH, HUD, AND SALEH (A.S)

AN EXPLORATION INTO QURANIC EXEGESIS BY QURAN

TRUTH SEEKERS FOUNDATION
MELBOURNE, AUSTRALIA

CONTENTS

PREFACE

Dear brothers and sisters, this book marks the second instalment in the series titled "Prophets and Prophethood (*Risalat w Nabuwwat*)". As you may recall, our primary intent and focus of this series, is to gain insights through the interconnected study of Quranic verses or *Tafseer* of Quran by Quran. It is widely known but less acknowledged, that a vast majority of Muslims are unaware of Quranic concepts and oblivious to the framework of *Marefat* laid down in the Holy Text. Therefore, by emphasizing on understanding Quran by collating and organizing apparently dispersed verses, we not only aim to deepen our understanding of its richness and depth but also to recognize the gaps and deficiencies in our connection with the Divine Book. Quran must be the central and core reference for our *Deen*, which regrettably, is not the practice presently.

Prophethood has manifested itself along two major avenues. The first offers 'Ideological and Practical guidance on *Towheed* and *Akherat*.' The second provides a comprehensive and consolidated system of living in this world in a manner that enables humans to earn respect and love of their Creator accompanied by a blissful eternal life. Every Prophet diligently toiled for these objectives and sacrificed their every asset to emancipate humanity from the chains and prisons of ignorance and darkness (جہالت اور ظلم). The sad reality entailing these noble efforts of Prophets is the ferocious and rebellious resistance of the elites of society followed by the indifference and cowardice of the masses in supporting the truth. The entire history of Prophethood is fraught with such conflicts, culminating in many instances into the infliction of Divine wrath or *Azab-e-Ilahi.* (عذاب الہی)

In this volume, we shall discuss the Quranic narratives of three Prophets sent for human guidance before Hazrat Ibrahim (a.s): Hazrat Nooh, Hud, and Saleh (a.s). Why are the events of these three Prophets combined together in a single volume? Because these three nations and their character carry some striking resemblances, which we will explore in the light of Quranic discourses. The most important commonality was the occurrence of extremely abnormal events (عذاب الہی) that ultimately destroyed them all. These arrogant nations succumbed to a fate after which there was no opportunity for return in *Dunya* and no respite and solace in *Akherat*.

As we delve into these discussions, we will uncover numerous lessons and guidelines pertinent to our lives. It is our sincere hope that readers will appreciate our analytical approach to studying Quran and find fulfillment in discovering the patterns within the Divine text. The ultimate satisfaction will be achieved when the readers acquire the intelligence and acumen to extract the patterns embedded in the Divine text. I pray that with Allah's Help you will gradually develop this ability of connecting the Quranic meanings by piecing together various verses, thereby decoding, unlocking, and enjoying the Divine Message.

May Allah help us all in becoming what He has chosen us to be.

Sincere prayers of Blessings of Dunya and Akherat for all of you.

Syed Haider Riza
Melbourne, Australia.

CHAPTER 1

PRE-ABRAHAMIC PROPHETS NOOH, HUD AND SALEH (A.S)

1.1. BACKGROUND AND INTRODUCTION

From the time of Hazrat Adam, humanity has grown exponentially. The shocking event of *Habeel* murdered by his brother *Qabeel*, starkly revealed that this new species, freshly arrived on earth, has a fair share of its own problems. From the outset, human life was neither easy nor smooth, it was brimming with hardships and struggles, both internal, within the soul, and external, relating to the world and other humans. Humanity's journey began to resemble the strenuous pursuits of a wanderer in the rugged mountains or a surfer navigating the ferocious ocean waves, rising and falling with their crests and troughs.

Despite all the looming troubles and perils, the encouraging and soothing aspect was Allah's ever present guiding role in human life. How can we be sure of that? Through the appearance of continual guidance in the form of chosen human beings whom we know as the Prophets of Allah (پیامبران الهی). Following Hazrat Adam, several Prophets emerged among whom the most important was Hazrat Idrees known as *Ukhnu* or Enoch in the Hebrew language. The exact number of years, spent by those early Prophets on Earth, assigned the responsibility of spreading *Hidayat,* is unknown.

However, this fact remained undeniable that most humans were averse to the message of Allah and preferred a life punctuated by unfettered lusts and vicious desires. Gradually the situation deteriorated to the extent that a Divine decree became inevitable for a final showdown. It means that the humanity would be given a final but sufficiently prolonged opportunity to reform themselves failing which they will be banished from the face of earth and replaced by a "new" humanity. Thus, began the era of Hazrat Nooh (a.s).

Hazrat Nooh was born during a critical and precarious epoch of humanity, which, only ten to twelve generations after its inception, was unknowingly facing an existential threat. Granted an exceptionally long life, Hazrat Nooh (a.s) offered numerous opportunities of repentance to the human generations or civilization existing at that time. Unfortunately, darkness within the souls prevailed and those chances were not availed. Ultimately, the inevitable cataclysm transpired in the form of an unprecedented deluge sweeping the cities and towns with unparalleled intensity and ferocity. In the post flood era, only Hazrat Nooh and his three sons survived with their wives. This small family was crowned with the status of the original ancestors, grand forefathers and root of modern humanity.

The subsequent phase of humanity witnessed the rise of powerful nations highly adept in building strong and articulate structures. This was the era of the nations of *Aad* and *Thamud*, described in Quran as the builders of extraordinary cities in deserts and carvers of their dwellings from rocky mountains. Although the eras of *Aad* and *Thamud* did not overlap, with *Thamud* arriving later, they were close enough in time to be aware of their predecessor's history. Despite their technological prowess, these nations indulged in sinful lifestyles, preferring tyranny and bigotry over Divine submission and kindness towards fellow human beings. The problems of idol worshipping, usurpation of others' rights and blatant immorality became rampant in their societies. Once again, the humanity was flirting with grave dangers.

The Mercy and Grace of Allah still persisted and did not leave the humanity to rot and decay in the filth of devilish behaviours. Prophet Hud was sent towards the nation of *Aad* and later on Hazrat Saleh was given the responsibility of guiding *Thamud*. Despite the most diligent and persistent efforts of these great Prophets to inspire positive reformations in their respective nations, their preachings too, went in vain and both the nations, like those before them were eventually annihilated. It is a very important fact to note that it was the earliest humanity who faced the destructive punishment (عذاب) more than the later generations. From the times of Hazrat *Lut* onwards, while punishment and destruction did descend upon the nations, there were survivors from those nations as well. It was not like eradicating a whole nation from the face of earth.

There are many narrations and stories about this second phase of humanity – post Hazrat Nooh - but in keeping with our commitment to the Quranic text and context, we will not delve any deeper into historical details of early humanity, which anyways, is flimsy and largely unverified. Now, we focus on the introduction of the contents to be discussed in this volume.

1.2. OVERVIEW OF THE BOOK

You now hold the second volume of **Know Your Quran series**, where we shall discuss and extract life-improving lessons from Quranic verses related to the three most significant Prophets who lived before Hazrat Ibrahim (a.s). We are fortunate that Allah has enlightened us about those noble souls from antiquity, sharing insights into their Prophetic lives and the conduct of their nations, for our maximum understanding. You should have anticipated by the discussion in the previous section that these Prophets are Hazrat Nooh, Hud, and Saleh (a.s). Despite the time gap of over two thousand years between them and the revelation of Quran, Allah has deemed their remembrance (*zikr*) relevant and significant enough to be described for us in appreciable detail across at least fourteen Surahs of the Holy Quran. Among them, Hazrat Nooh holds peculiar significance due to two main reasons, his extraordinary age, and his eventual role as the progenitor of modern humanity.

You might wonder why in a single volume we have combined the descriptions of three Prophets. The rationale is twofold. Firstly, the Quranic discussion about Hazrat Hud and Saleh is not detailed enough to warrant a separate book. Second and more importantly, the era from Hazrat Nooh to Saleh bears significant resemblance. It is marked by the stubborn denial of people to accept and submit to the Divine message. The nations of these three Prophets, despite being blessed with great material power and wealth persistently confronted their Prophets until they came face to face with the *Azab* plunging them into ruin and destruction. All these nations faced devastating Divine retributions.

This book follows a similar pattern established in volume 1, on Hazrat Adam (a.s); of accurate verse translation followed by the explanation of important concepts and elucidating further through thought-provoking questions. However, this volume bears a slight difference in that some deeper important lessons are extracted and elaborated in detail under separate headings at the end of every chapter. This will help in probing the wisdom embedded in the verses with better insight. Not restricted to the explanation section, conspicuous effort is also made to directly highlight and illustrate the meanings that continue to emerge as we move along the flow of Quranic verses.

Our discussion focusses on uncovering the templates of Divine knowledge by exploring the patterns embedded in Quranic verses. It is crucial to understand that Quran does not tell stories but illuminates the 'Truth' through narration of lives and events. Quran is revealed in a manner that facilitates the extraction and formulation of patterns, which elucidate rules governing both human and universal life. These patterns and models encompass the entire spectrum of beliefs and actions that either draw humans closer to Allah for His Blessings or, conversely, lead them to perdition in case of denial and rejection. The Quran is filled with enlightening ideas, and by adjusting our vantage point in accordance with the Divine guidance, the Light becomes visible. We sincerely hope that this effort of bringing *Tafseer* of the Holy Quran will significantly assist our dear readers in developing these visionary skills.

CHAPTER 2
HAZRAT NOOH (A.S)

2.1. IMPORTANT FACTS

1. Hazrat Nooh (a.s) is the first among the **Ulul Azm** Prophets. *Ulul Azm* are those prophets who enjoy maximum proximity to Allah and can be regarded as the chiefs of all the Prophets. Their main characteristic is that Allah has bestowed them with the *Shariah*. Their names are **Nooh, Ibrahim, Moosa, Isa and Mohammad (s.a.w)**.

Q.1. What is the meaning of *Shariah*?

A: *Shariah* literally refers to a clear and expansive pathway leading to water in a lake or river. In the language of religion, *Shariah* is the comprehensive and unambiguous set of rules that govern the individual and social lives of the believers, offering a clear and broad pathway leading to eternal salvation. These rules and regulations are not crafted by the Prophets; instead, these are besstowed by Allah through the 'chosen ones among the Prophets'. The first person obligated to obey and follow the dictates of *Shariah* is the Prophet himself. Those Prophets who deliver *Shariah* to humanity are known as *Rasool*.

2. Hazrat Nooh (a.s) was granted an extraordinarily long life by Allah for a specific purpose. Historical accounts vary on his life span, but he certainly lived on this earth for over 1000 years, around approximately 5000 years

ago. While some theories suggest that such a life span might have been normal back then, there is no concrete evidence to substantiate such claims. This leads us to consider the duration of the earthly life of Hazrat Nooh as a miracle.

3. Hazrat Nooh preached his nation, and probably to all the existing nations in that era, for 950 years. This number is told to us by the Quran himself in Sura *Ankaboot* (29).

4. Hazrat Nooh is regarded as the second Adam and is considered as the father of the modern human race. Why? Because during his time, all humanity - except for those who were saved alongside him - was eradicated by the great flood. Therefore, the humanity we see today has descended from his three sons.

5. Hazrat Nooh built an extraordinary Ark or Ship, that not only survived the great flood but was also spacious enough to accommodate and carry all the animal species to safety.

6. One of Hazrat Nooh's wives and one of his sons were non-believers and could not escape the *Azab* of Allah. It proves that being related to a sacred person does not guarantee *Iman* or *Jannah*; rather, every individual must earn their *Iman* and act in accordance with *Shariah* to receive Allah's blessings. The Quranic reference for the *Azab* upon wife of Hazrat Nooh is Surah *Tehreem*, V. 10.

7. Hazrat Nooh endured extremely long periods of abuse and torture from his nation but never turned away from expressing his gratitude (*shukr*) to Allah and praying for the misguided, until he became convinced that now no one else would believe. That's why Allah has remembered him in the

Quran as an extremely grateful *Abd* of Allah. (*Abd e Shakoor* – Sura *Asra* V. 3)

8. After centuries of preaching, Hazrat Nooh found only a small group of believers (*momineen*) - less than 100 people, aside from his family - who believed in his message and cause. These few individuals were the survivors who managed to evade the devastating impact of flood by boarding the Ark.

9. The humanity after Hazrat Adam was fraught with some grave problems, the killing of one brother by his real brother, being among the most heinous. Hazrat Nooh emerged as the source to purge humanity from all original evils. His descendants spread across the earth embodying a new era without mutual enmity, hatred, immorality, and with the granted blessings of Allah as we shall observe in verses of Sura Hud.

10. The life of Hazrat Nooh clearly demonstrates that it is not possible to defeat or eliminate the system of Allah through wealth or power of government. Allah always finds a way to prevail and ensures the triumph and safety of His Prophets.

2.2. STUDY AND ANALYSIS OF QURANIC VERSES DESCRIBING THE EVENTS OF THE LIFE OF HAZRAT NOOH (A.S)

In total, 14 Surahs in Quran mention Hazrat Nooh or describe the events related to his extraordinary life. Sura Hud (11) and Sura Nooh (71), in particular, provide considerable details about his life, preaching, and key events. In our study, we shall mainly refer to verses in these two Surahs for gaining valuable information and insights during our analysis.

Sura Hud (11)

In this surah the events of Hazrat Nooh are described from the initiation of his mission of inviting people towards Allah (*dawah*) till the conclusion of the flood. This Sura is unique in that it is the only one in Quran where the issue of the drowned son of Hazrat Nooh is discussed. Unlike Hazrat Moosa and Hazrat Isa there are no details provided about Hazrat Nooh's birth. The description of the events of Hazrat Nooh begins from verse 25.

V. 25: "Indeed, We sent Nooh towards his nation and he said to them, "Surely I am a clear and open warner (نذير) for you."

> **Addressing an anomaly:** Verse 25 is saying that Allah has sent Hazrat Nooh towards his nation. This is puzzling since Hazrat Nooh was living in his nation. Hence, it cannot be a physical relocation, so what else? This phrase highlights an important fact about Prophethood: when Allah chooses a human as His Prophet, that individual is elevated to higher levels of Malakoot (ملكوت), where he acquires *Ilm e ladunni* (علم اللدنى) or Godly knowledge. From that exalted state, the Prophet is asked to return to his people to share with them the knowledge of religion (*Deen*) of Allah in matters of faith (*Iman*) and action (*Amal*), both.

Q 2. Who is Warner (Nazeer) in Quranic terms?

A: Human beings are the wayfarers. They are traveling from *Dunya* to *Akherat*, a journey which is perilous and precarious. Therefore, a sincere and truthful guide is essential to navigate this journey successfully. A *Nazeer* (warner), in Quranic perspective, is someone- Prophet or Imam or their true disciples- who is aware of all the complexities related to the life's journey and alerts people to the impending dangers and pitfalls they will face. A *Nazeer* not only elucidates these dangers through verbal teachings but also offers practical guidance towards paths of safety and security. While his language may at times feel harsh, in fact, his every advice is based on love and sincerity, with a fervent desire to protect people from the snares of the devil and the dangers of their journey.

Q 3. How is a Prophet *Nazeer?*

A: In our earthly existence, humans not only face bodily or physical dangers but also threats to their souls and intellect, which are numerous and far more formidable. On one side, they are continually allured by their mischievous and untrained soul (نفس امّاره) while on the other, incessantly bombarded and threatened by the whispers (وسواس) of *shaytan* and his tribe. These internal and external enemies combine and contrive to distract humans from acquiring the righteous and virtuous morals (اخلاق حسنہ) and lure them into sinning. The Prophet acts as a watchful and vigilant guardian, cautioning and reprimanding those journeying the 'path of life' about its perilous bends, deadly traps, and the routes surrounded by thieves and robbers. Prophet, as *Nazeer*, continuously warns the people about the malevolent and deceitful tactics of *shaytan*, which represents the greatest hazard in human life. As a *Nazeer* he persistently reminds them that although the journey is inevitable and fraught with dangers, it can be safely traversed by adhering to the Divine Guidance."

The preaching of Hazrat Nooh (a.s) continued in verse 26:

V. 26: (I warn you) not to do *Bandagi* of anyone except Allah. Certainly, I fear for you the *Azab* of a painful day.

Q 4. What is the painful day Hazrat Nooh is referring to?

A: This refers to the judgment day or *Qeyamah* which can be very painful for those who sin and who are not sincere *Abd* of Allah. On that day the ruling of *"What you do is what you get"* would be paramount. Some people tend to accept the notion that the powerful people or sanctified personalities may rescue them on the day of *Qeyamah* like what is observed on many occasions in this world. Nay! No such possibility exists since no one except those permitted by Allah will have the opportunity to intercede (شفاعت) on that day, and the ones blessed with Allah's permission will never advocate for those whom Allah disapproves. --

Hazrat Nooh's *Dawah* apparently fell on deaf ears and met with a scornful response from the influential people of his nation, as recounted in verse 27 of Sura Hud (11):

V. 27: Then the disbelieving chiefs from his (Nooh's) nation said, "(i) We see you nothing more than a *Bashar* (human) like us and (ii) we do not see your followers except that they are the lowest among us, in status and without any credibility. (iii) And we do not observe any merit and preference for you over us; (iv) (Conclusion) instead, we think that you are liars."

Q 5: It is mostly observed that the Prophets of Allah were fiercely opposed by the wealthy and authoritative people in their nation. Is it a continuing trend, and if so, why?

A: It is an aspect that is most worthy of careful scrutiny and pondering. Prophets invariably faced fierce resistance from those in power, who possessed material wealth and higher social status. The main reasons that could be cited for the enmity of the materially powerful against the *Dawah* of prophets are: (i) the invitation to *Towheed* naturally commands for demolition of existing power centres propped up by the tyrants and usurpers of the national wealth. Consequently, the preaching of Prophets emerges as the imminent and most serious threat to their hegemony and status quo of the supremacy of few over the majority. (ii) the Prophets' message of uplifting and honouring the poor demands sacrifice and investment from the wealthy, and (iii) the Shariah laws do not encourage a small elite to grab maximum wealth and authority, instead they advocate for equitable distribution of resources among all the sections of humanity; a proposition repugnant to those who have already seized the society's assets for their personal gains.

THE PATTERN BEHIND TYRANTS' OPPOSITION TO THE *DAWAH* OF HAZRAT NOOH.

The influential and powerful in Hazrat Nooh's nation immediately became engaged in the act of fiercely opposing his preaching. This outburst followed a recurring pattern, a template consistently adopted by tyrants (طاغوت) till today. This pattern can be dissected and illustrated as follows:

a) **No intellectual content or weightage:** The elite and influential groups in Hazrat Nooh's nation responded to his *dawah* with almost spontaneous and vehement opposition. Rather than engaging in an intellectual debate or questioning the foundations of Hazrat Nooh's call to *Towheed* and taking heed of accountability on Judgment Day, they chose a different tactic. Their criticism and attacks were not aimed at comprehending the content of Hazrat Nooh's message itself. Instead, they focused on criticising Hazrat Nooh and his followers among the believers (momineen) by targeting their social standing and apparent status.

b) **Discrediting the opponent leader:** The tyrants attacked Hazrat Nooh's credibility on two fronts. Firstly, they dismissed him as a mere human, indistinguishable from themselves and hence, declared him ineligible or incapable of receiving Divine revelation. According to their deceptive logic, only a super-human being could connect to the heavens. Secondly, they argued that lack of material supremacy and high status automatically undermined his worthiness of attention. Since Hazrat Nooh did not belong to the elites, therefore, carry no weight to be considered important and worthy of listening.

c) **Disparaging the Opposition:** The influential tyrants within Hazrat Nooh's nation resorted to outright dismissal of those who embraced *Iman* through his teachings, by categorizing them as the scum of the society solely due to their lack of wealth. This approach to evaluating individuals' worth on the basis of wealth is a deeply flawed and contemptible practice. It reflects a gross misunderstanding of human value, reducing it to mere financial terms and ignoring the intrinsic worth of individuals and their faith.

d) **Denouncing Opponents as Liars and Enemies of the Society:** The concluding sentence of the verse, where they declared Hazrat Nooh and the *momineen* as liars, unveils their true intent: to utterly reject and suppress the Divine message and its advocates. By the end of verse, it is evident that the lords and chiefs opposing Hazrat Nooh were entirely disinterested in comprehending Allah's message, accepting the truth, and following the path of justice.

HAZRAT NOOH'S RESPONSE

In response to their tirade, Hazrat Nooh did not remain silent, rather, he forcefully and eloquently refuted their accusations and clearly articulated his own position.

V. 28: He (Nooh) replied: "O my nation! Have you seen (gave attention to the fact) that if I am upon clear evidence (or possess clear signs) from my Rab and He has granted me mercy from Himself, yet you have blinded yourself from that? (In that case) can I force (*Hidayat*) upon you when you are averse to it?"

V. 29: "And my nation, I do not ask you for any wealth in exchange for it [conveying to you the Divine message]. I do not see my reward upon anyone but Allah, and I am not going to drive away the believers. Indeed, they meet their Rab, and I view you as an ignorant nation.

Q 6. What is the clear evidence that a Prophet carries with him?

A: The clear signs referred to by Hazrat Nooh in verse 28 are in fact, observable in every prophet of Allah. The teachings offered by the Prophets are logical, intellectually appealing, and verifiable through various checks and balances. The main aspects of their teachings are invariably focussed on encouraging and guiding every individual towards becoming God-fearing and honest. The second proof is the personal character of every Prophet which represents the exemplification of truthfulness and trustworthiness. Thirdly, the Prophets never ask for any return or reward from the people except the sincere *Bandagi* of Allah and adherence to His Will and teachings.

DR. SYED HAIDER RIZA

THE ELEVATION OF MOMINEEN THROUGH DIVINE GUIDANCE (*HIDAYAT*)

The last sentence in verse 29 of Sura Hud (11) speaks of a very strange occurrence - the meeting of momineen with their Rab. This is immensely inspiring and motivating for anyone who embraces the true message of Allah. Therefore, it is appropriate to explain a few concepts related to the *Hidayat* which elevates the *momineen* nearer to their Rab.

a) *Hidayat* cannot be enforced nor based on self-concocted assumptions of the people. It is an illumination of the soul, a heavenly gift granted by Allah to those who prove their eligibility for its reception. There are very specific and strict conditions or requirements to be a recipient of Divine *Hidayat*. In addition, there are peculiar signs that manifest themselves as conclusive proof in a person who has successfully received *Hidayat* from Allah. Those clear signs as mentioned by our Holy Prophet include experiencing sweetness of Allah's zikr, detachment of heart from everything perishable and yearning for the world of true life and eternity (ذکر الٰہی، زہد اور فنا ہونے والی نعمتوں سے بے رغبتی)

b) *Hidayat* is accompanied by the transformation of the state of soul (*Nafs*). The person whose heart attains and absorbs *Hidayat* becomes a *momin* in the true sense. Such an individual develops a live connection with his or her Rab through which Godly inspirations flow into their souls, continually enriching and enlightening them.

c) The tyrants opposing the Prophets and *Deen* consider the true *momineen* as their adversaries and therefore, apply maximum efforts to dismantle and disorganize them. However, as Hazrat Nooh had elucidated in verse 29, every *momin* enjoys a personal bond with his or her Rab while the Prophet acting as the channel through which the *momin* receives guidance and directions to spend a Godly life. *This is a very important fact that Prophethood is established by Allah to generate and maintain the personal connection of humans with their Creator and Rab.*

HAZRAT NOOH'S *DAWAH* AND HIS NATION'S RESPONSE

Here we shall momentarily pause the discussion on verses of Sura Hud and turn our attention to verses from Sura Nooh (71) which emphasize upon the essence of the *dawah* of Hazrat Nooh (a.s) and his approach in preaching to his nation. It is truly remarkable how Hazrat Nooh spent such a long time persistently imploring his people to accept *Iman* and come out of their wretchedness. Sura Nooh, the 71st Sura of Quran and named in the honour of this great Prophet, recounts Hazrat Nooh's interactions with his wickedly defiant nation. It vividly portrays his love-filled entreaties to them, urging them to embrace Allah's mercy and seek their deliverance.

Sura Nooh (71)

V. 1: Indeed, We sent Nooh towards his nation (with the instructions) that "Warn your people before a painful *Azab* comes to them."

V. 2: He (complied) and said, "O my nation! Surely, I am a clear warner (*Nazeer*) for you."

V. 3: "(and) that you worship Allah [become His *abd*] and observe His *Taqwa* and obey me."

V. 4: "He will grant you *maghferat* from your sins and reprieve you (with goodness) till an appointed time. Indeed, when Allah's appointed time arrives no one (has the capacity) to delay it, if only you have (appropriate) knowledge."

Faced by a scornful response from his nation Hazrat Nooh turned to His Rab for help and support.

V.5: Nooh said, "O my Rab! Surely, I pleaded to my nation (during) day and night."

V.6: "But my calling increased nothing but their fleeing away from me."

V.7: "And whenever I invited them so that you (O Allah) grant them *Maghferat* they press their fingers into their ears and wrapped (their faces) with their clothes and persisted (in their denial) and exhibited great arrogance."

V.8: "(But still) I continued my *dawah* openly (in the broad daylight)."

V.9: "Then certainly I called them publicly and privately and in secrecy."

V.10: "saying to them, 'Ask for the *Maghferat* of your Rab, He is certainly *Ghaffar*."

V.11: "He will shower you with abundant rain."

V.12: "And strengthen you with the wealth and sons and give you the gardens and bless you with lakes."

INVITATION TOWARDS *TAQWA* AND *MAGHFERAT*:

a) Verse 3 of this sura encapsulates the core principles of life as a *momin*. It emphasizes three key aspects: (i) *bandagi* of Allah (ii) *Taqwa* and God consciousness; and (iii) unwavering obedience and submission to the messenger of Allah. These elements form the essence and crux of the Divine message delivered by the Prophets and reiterated numerous times in the Quran under different contexts.

b) The first ten verses of Sura Nooh vividly depict the profound love and immense compassion of a Prophet for his people. Hazrat Nooh literally consumed himself for guiding his people towards salvation. He relentlessly and wholeheartedly delivered Allah's message seizing every opportunity without caring about day or night. But alas, despite his most sincere *dawah*, his people continuously disregarded him and drifted further away from the path he urged them to follow.

c) Hazrat Nooh persistently encouraged his people towards *Maghferat* of Allah (verse 10 Sura Nooh) which is the most important blessing in the life of a Muslim and *momin*. *Maghferat* signifies not only forgiveness but also cleansing of the soul from the filthy roots and poisonous effects of sinning. This concept will be explored further in this chapter.

d) Hazrat Nooh also made it clear to his nation that accepting *Iman*, embracing *Taqwa,* and following a pious life is not only a guarantee for prosperous *Akherat* but also opens the doors to the bounties of heavens and blissful resources of the earth in this life. This critical truth highlights that if a nation or communities dedicate themselves to a life of *Iman* and *Taqwa*, they not only secure rewards of *Akherat* but are also blessed with abundant rain and food for an affluent and prosperous life in this earthly abode.

e) The manner in which Hazrat Nooh approached his nation and persuaded them to leave the life of *kufr* is heart-melting. This shows the immense love for the *bandegan* of Allah which His appointed representative, Nabi, or Imam, cherishes in his heart. Despite continuous rejection, Hazrat Nooh never exhibited any slackness or laziness in his efforts to attract and pull the people towards the salvation offered through the *Maghferat* of Allah.

HAZRAT NOOH'S HELPLESSNESS IN HIS NATION

Following numerous altercations between Hazarat Nooh and the lords of his nation, the conflict remained unresolved and increasingly Hazrat Nooh found himself alienated, culminating in a state of loneliness and helplessness within his nation. This distressing phase of his life is poignantly captured in these three verses of Sura Shu'ara (26).

Sura Shu'ara (26)

V. 116: They (the nation of Nooh) threatened, "If you do not desist (from your *dawah*), certainly and surely you will be among those stoned (to death)."

V.117: Hazrat Nooh (cried to his Rab), "O my Rab! Surely my nation has thoroughly and vehemently rejected me."

V.118: "Thus, judge between me and them decisively, and relieve me and those who are accompanying me (on the path of truth) from the *momineen*."

This pivotal phase in the closing stages of Hazrat Nooh's preaching is also captured in verse 32 of Sura Hud and verses 9 & 10 of Sura Qamar (54). Let us have a look at Sura Qamar:

Sura Qamar (54)

V. 9: Before them (the infidels of Arabia), the nation of Nooh had forcefully denied and thoroughly rejected our *Abd* and declared him insane.

V. 10: Thus, he (Nooh) prayed to his Rab, "I am overwhelmed, so help me!"

These verses unequivocally depict Hazrat Nooh's despair, as he endured the disdain of his people, ultimately seeking solace and a final resolution of his troubles from Allah. Critical juncture in this long chain of events arrived when these people brazenly demanded Hazrat Nooh to manifest the Divine punishment (*Azab*) he had forewarned. That state was a testament to their deep rooted *kufr* and the intensity of Hazrat Nooh's trials as a Prophet of Allah.

PLIGHT OF THE NATION OF HAZRAT NOOH

Hazrat Nooh was extremely unfortunate in that his nation exhibited extreme reluctance in listening to his *dawah* and responded with every fiendish plot they could hatch. Facing such implacable opposition, Hazrat Nooh prayed Allah to terminate this vicious hegemony, a plea that, tragically, could only be fulfilled by their annihilation. The following verses of Sura Nooh (71) detail the egregious actions of Hazrat Nooh's nation, his plea for deliverance and his prayer for the eradication of those who were irredeemably defiant and unrepentant.

Sura Nooh (71)

V. 21: And Nooh said, "O my Rab! Indeed they (his nation) have disobeyed me and followed those who increased nothing but loss for them in their offspring and wealth.

V. 22: And they devised tremendously devious schemes (against me).

V. 23: And they exhorted (their followers): "Never ever abandon your gods and (especially) never forsake *Wadd, Suwa, Yaguth, Yaooq and Nasr*."

V. 24: Hazrat Nooh continued his lamentation to Allah, "And (that's how) these (chiefs and lords) led a lot of people astray. Thus, (O my Rab) do not increase anything but further deviation (from the right path) for the *zalimeen*."

V. 25: (the prayers of Hazrat Nooh were fulfilled and): Due to their sins and wrongdoings, **they were drowned and entered the hell fire,** finding no helper but Allah.

The concluding verses of the Surah mention Hazrat Nooh's prayer for complete banishment of the pillars of *kufr* from the face of this earth; **a wish yet to be fulfilled.**

V. 26: And prayed Nooh, "O my Rab! Do not leave a single home of *kafereen* (settled) on the earth."

V. 27: "Surely, if You spare them, they will misguide and de-track your *bandegan* and raise only the wicked sinners and staunch *kafereen* in their progeny."

Reflecting upon this narrative, we earnestly pray that Allah completely detach and dissociate all of us from indulging in any form and type of *haram* and honour this *Dua* of Hazrat Nooh to alleviate the sufferings and tribulations inflicted upon humanity by the servants of *Taghoot*.

Explanation:

1. Hazrat Nooh was acutely aware that rejecting his *dawah* and befriending evil persons will invite divine punishment and the impending *Azab* would obliterate all the worldly possessions and relationships of people. It is the rule of life that living against *Iman*

and pursuing *shirk* and *kufr* brings nothing but the destruction of *Dunya* and *Akherat*.

2. Hazrat Nooh overwhelmed with grief and sorrow, finally expressed his distress to Allah. He supplicated, "O Allah! For year after year, I kept on following them tirelessly with request after request to embrace *Iman* and seek Your Mercy. Yet, all I received in return was conspiracy, malice, and plots for my destruction."

3. In verse 23, the last five names refer to the fabricated names of idols worshipped by this nation as gods. The specific mention of their names suggests that among the pantheon of false gods, these idols held a special status.

4. Verse 24 signifies a remarkable moment when Hazrat Nooh, for the first time, implored Allah not for guidance (*Hidayat*) but for the further deviation (ضلالت) of the unjust people (ظالمین) from the truth. This plea from the noble tongue of Hazrat Nooh reflects a profound fact: beyond a certain threshold of *zalalat*, sinners and transgressors cross into the realm of Allah's wrath (غضب الہی), resulting in their hearts becoming darkened and sealed against truth and Divine light.

5. The ultimate decree of *Azab* on this accursed nation materialized as a catastrophic flood, with salvation available only through the Ark of Allah. This was a fate these *kafer* people could not escape, as during their lives, when they had their choices, they denied and dismissed the loving Hand of Allah extended to them with *Rehmat* and *Maghferat*.

6. In verse 25, the depiction of the nation drowning in the flood water and then instantly entering hellfire is highly thought-provoking. It

emphasizes the notion that the destiny of *kafer* and *mushrik* is destruction, irrespective of the medium or means of their demise. Water, instead of giving them life, leads to their doom, and fire, far from offering warmth, ushers them into further punishment.

TERMINAL PUNISHMENT (*AZAB*) FOR THE NATION AND SALVATION FOR MOMINEEN

Once the hearts are sealed, the possibility of spiritual recovery fades away. This was the case with the nation of Hazrat Nooh, who ironically, themselves demanded the punishment of Allah. The gradual hardening of their hearts, leading them inexorably towards the ultimate destructive *Azab* can be studied in the following verses of Sura Hud, which describe these events in detail and are self-explanatory.

Sura Hud (11)

V. 32: They (those who were quarrelling with Nooh) said, "O Nooh, surely you have disputed and argued with us extensively. Now bring upon us what you threaten if you are (really) among the truthful ones."

These words deeply saddened Hazrat Nooh. As a Prophet, he recognized the irreparable and irreversible state of these people's souls, foreseeing their inevitable destiny to face the wrath of Allah. It is a stark and frightening observation that all nations sentenced to the ultimate destruction had in fact, demanded *Azab* themselves and challenged the prophet to realize his warnings.

Soon, the final Word came from the Almighty.

V. 36: And this *Wahi* was sent to Nooh that now no one will accept *Iman* from your nation except those who had already believed. Thus, do not feel distressed by whatever they are doing.

Q 7: Who sent this message to Hazrat Nooh about no further men or women accepting *Iman*?

A: Allah sent His final verdict once the hearts of the nation of Hazrat Nooh were sealed off from absorbing any sane advice. This revelation also served as a definitive directive for Hazrat Nooh to alert the *momineen* and begin his preparations before the impending *Azab* on his nation.

Next, came one of the most extraordinary directives ever issued to a Prophet in the whole history of Prophethood: to build a vessel capable of surviving an unprecedented storm and flood while carrying some humans and a couple of pairs of every animal species living on earth!

V. 37: "And construct or build the Ark before our Eyes, per our Revelation and do not address Me regarding those who are unjust. Indeed, they are drowned."

Q 8: Why was Hazrat Nooh instructed to build the Ark under Allah's supervision?

A: The Ark's functionality and performance were meant to be extraordinary, surpassing human capabilities. This sentence implied that the job was beyond every human skill and needed divine intervention. The construction of the Ark was a project of unprecedented nature, unlike anything undertaken before and not to be replicated in the future. This unique endeavour, commanded by divine instruction, was not only novel in its concept but also in its scale and purpose.

V. 38: And he (Nooh) got busy building the ship and whenever the elites and leaders from his nation passed by, mocking, and ridiculing him, he replied, "If you are mocking us now, then surely we shall ridicule you (one day) as you debase us (now)."

V. 39: "And you will know that who will be inflicted with a disgraceful punishment and upon whom an *Azab* will descend that shall not go away."

Finally, after an appreciably long wait, during which Nooh was perfecting the Ark according to Allah's instructions the instant arrived when water started gushing out from the oven, signalling the start of flood.

V. 40: Until when our Order came, and the oven busted and overflowed. We said, "Load in the Ark each of the two pairs (from animals) and mates and your family except the one for whom my word is already decreed and those who have accepted *Iman* (so far)." And none had believed with him except very few.

V. 41: And he (Nooh) said, "Board it or embark therein, With the *Ism e Allah* is its cruising and anchoring. Indeed, my Rab is *Ghafoor* and *Raheem*."

INHABITANTS OF HAZRAT NOOH'S ARK

a) A greatly diverse array of creatures/species boarded Nooh's Ark which became a source of safeguarding them from the devastating *Azab* of the great flood. Prominent among them were the family of Hazrat Nooh, but as told in Quranic verses, even within Nooh's family, some were excluded from the final salvation. As transpired at the boarding time, the lost ones included one of his wives and a son.

b) In addition to his family, a small number of believers, as told in verse 40, joined Nooh on the Ark. Some *Riwayat* mention the number of believers boarding the Ark to be 80 only.

c) Allah commanded Hazrat Nooh to take with him two pairs of every animal species on board. This directive was given to preserve those species, ensuring their continuation and reproduction after the flood receded and life on earth could resume towards normalcy.

DROWNING OF SON BEFORE HIS EYES

The Quranic narrative of Hazrat Nooh in Sura Hud (11) concludes with a particularly poignant and unique episode, an event which involves the drowning of one of his own sons.

V. 42: And it (the Ark) sailed with them (people and animals) in the waves which were like mountains and Nooh called his son when he was moving away from the ship, "O my son! Come aboard with us and do not remain with the *kafereen*."

V. 43: He (son) replied, "I will soon take refuge towards a mountain which will protect me from the water." He (Nooh) admonished him, "There is no protector this day from the decree of Allah, except for whom Allah grants His mercy." (And this discourse was not finished) when a wave surged between them, and he (the son) was among the drowned ones.

This incident is significant as it highlights the subtle themes of Divine Will, the limitations of human perception, and the profound trials faced by Prophets in their missions. Hazrat Nooh's experience with his son serves as a reminder of the ultimate authority of Allah's decisions, His unwavering principles and the distinction between familial ties and the cardinal importance of faithfulness (صالحیت وایمان).

ENDING OF FLOOD AND WONDERFUL ELOQUENCE OF V. 44

After tormenting cities and dwellings, the unprecedented *Azab* in the form of a great flood was over and normalcy gradually returned. Verse 44 of Sura Hud (11) is one of the most eloquent verses in *Quran e Kareem* and beautifully captures the cessation of the catastrophic event and subsequent commencement of a new phase of existence.

V.44: And it was said, "O earth! Swallow up your water and O sky! Withhold (your rain) and (consequently) the water receded, and the decree fulfilled and (the Ark) rested and balanced on (the mountain) *Judi* and it was said, "Perish be the *zalimeen*."

In remarkably brief but immensely eloquent sentences this extraordinary verse lucidly describes six events in sequence that were executed once the Divine Decree (امر الہی) had decided to terminate the storm and flood. Every event represents one specific Order issued by Allah and faithfully executed by the relevant system without any resistance. Some of these were physical happenings in the material world and some relate to the functioning of the heavenly system controlling the earthly life. These synchronized events can be summarized as:

i.   The earth was ordered to 'swallow' the water that had flown out from its 'belly or inside'. This is a very strange fact since normally we do not experience any flood in which water sprouts from deep inside the earth or flows outwards from beneath the surface of the earth. However, in the case of Nooh's flood, the hidden subterranean water sources were also unleashed.

ii.   Intensely heavy rain falling from the skies was adding to the water on the earth gushing from inside. After Earth, the Divine directive came to the skies to put a stop to the torrential downpour.

iii.   Then the command came for all the water that was accumulated on the earth to move into certain corners and low-lying areas clearing main passages and major pathways and restoring the Earth's habitability.

iv.   The flood resulted in the elimination of all the tyrant chiefs and lords and everyone who preferred to follow those despots instead of the Prophet of Allah. Thus, the Decree of Allah was executed and enforced for every criminal resulting in their expulsion from all the worldly pleasures and being thrown into the torments of eternal hell. This is a universal decree that has been and will be executed for all the tyrants (*Taghooti* people) and systems and is not limited only to the era of Hazrat Nooh.

v.   It is mentioned in Quranic verses that the flood, once completely settled, resembled a raging sea with mountain-sized waves roaring forward and devouring everything in their way. Amidst this chaos, the Ark of Hazrat Nooh could be visualized as a piece of straw swaying randomly unable to navigate to any particular destination. It was nothing but a miracle that the Ark not only maintained its balance but steadily headed towards the top of a mountain named as *Judi* where it rested and anchored in a balanced manner without causing any harm to its passengers. This was the fifth command as given in the verse. Indeed, Allah never abandons His *bandegan* in any circumstance, regardless of how terrible or dreadful it may be.

vi.   Finally, the Order of doing away with the *zalimeen* or unjust people was enforced. This decree illustrates one of the core principles of universal life. Just as we observe in the human body, when the bodily system gets corrupted due to food poisoning or viral attack, instinctive and inherent actions are spontaneously taken by the body to purge the impure and restore the balance. Similarly, in the broader context of social life, infusion of *zulm* in any form inevitably leads to systemic corruption. In response, the system of life instinctively springs into corrective action resulting in purging off the *zalimeen*. This recurrent phenomenon is not accidental! It is decreed by Allah that *zalimeen* and *zulm* would never reign supreme over His creation.

HAZRAT NOOH'S EXEMPLARY OBEDIENCE AND RESPECT (ادب) BEFORE HIS RAB

The drowning Hazrat Nooh's son is indeed remarkable for two key reasons. Firstly, due to Hazrat Nooh's apparently puzzling stance of querying Allah about this incident. This inquiry stands out because it seems to contrast with Nooh's unwavering faith and profound understanding of Allah's Will. Secondly, his exemplary obedience and supreme *bandagi* in the midst of immense personal loss and grief. It is worth noting that since forewarned about the fate of one of his wives, Hazrat Nooh did not feel disturbed about her being left behind. In contrast, he was not anticipating his son to perish in the flood based on his understanding of Allah's assurance of protecting his family. If we continue with the verses of Sura Hud (11), we shall find Hazrat Nooh's dialogue with his Rab regarding his son's drowning:

V.45: And Nooh called his Rab and said, "O my Rab, indeed my son was from my family and certainly your Promise is truth, and You are the most just among all the judges."

V.46: (Allah) replied, "O Nooh! He (your son) was definitely not from your family (since) surely, he was a non-righteous act or conduct (عمل). Hence, do not ask me what you do not know about. I advise you (to abstain from such an act) lest you may become (someone) from the ignorant ones (جاهل).

Hazrat Nooh immediately retreated from his question and apologized in these words:

V.47: He said, "O my Rab, indeed I seek Your refuge in that I ask for something about which I have no knowledge; and if You don't grant me *Maghferat* and *Rehmat*, I shall be among the losers."

The preceding verses mention Hazrat Nooh inquiring Allah about his son's drowning. Without careful scrutiny, this query seems like a complaint or dissent. Since this aspect of the *seerah* of Hazrat Nooh (a.s) is widely misunderstood therefore, to clarify this misconception for our valued readers, we wish to delve a little deeper into this issue.

a) Initially, it is important to recognize that seeing one's son drowning before his eyes and tolerating the incident is an immensely painful ordeal. Yet, Hazrat Nooh's inquiry never meant to challenge Allah's decision but rather a quest for better comprehension. This was because Allah had promised to save the family of Hazrat Nooh, and outwardly this son did not appear to be among the disbelievers (کافرین).

b) Therefore, Allah's response came as an explanation followed by advice and a reminder rather than reprimand or scolding. This subtle point is commonly and conveniently ignored in *Tafseer* discussions concerning the plea of Hazrat Nooh to his Rab regarding the drowning of his son.

c) In verse 47, we observe the exemplary respect (ادب) of Hazrat Nooh when he immediately sought *Maghferat* of Allah upon sensing a hint of His displeasure towards his inquiry. These instances highlight the profound devotion and true beauty of *bandagi* of Allah's chosen ones; a greatness that transcends our feeble faith and confined intellect.

d) The final sentence in verse 46 serves as a stark reminder that for the chosen and elevated ones, even the slightest deviation from the norms of *bandagi* could create significant problems foremost of which is the darkness of ignorance.

END OF HAZRAT NOOH'S LIFE AND THE DAWN OF A NEW ERA FOR HUMANITY

After explaining the issue of his drowned son to, Allah guided Hazrat Nooh to move into a new post-flood life filled with His love and blessings, as mentioned in verse 48 of Sura Hud (11).

V. 48: And it was said (to Nooh) "Descend (from this mountain of Judi) with peace from Me and Blessings upon you and those who accompany you. And (for) the nations (in your posterity), We shall grant them the enjoyments (in this world) then they will receive painful punishment (عذاب) from us.

a) As expected, Nooh's life concluded with Divine Mercy and Blessings. Indeed, Hazrat Nooh deserved the love of Allah for his *bandagi* and perpetual gratefulness to his Rab despite going through such a tormenting course of life over a thousand years. He toiled day and night with utmost sincere efforts to prevent humanity from eternal damnation, enduring severe maltreatments meted out to him by his people, solely Allah's sake. In the third verse of Sura Asra (17), Allah has acknowledged Hazrat Nooh as the most grateful *Abd* (عبد شکور). Hazrat Nooh is the only Prophet decorated by this title in Quran.

b) The final sentence in verse 48 pre-informs Hazrat Nooh (a.s) that the people inhabiting the earth after him will not be much different from his own. After a brief stint of enjoying the worldly pleasures, they will also face the *Azab* of different nature due to their transgressions against the Divine.

2.3. THE PACKAGE OF *DEEN* GUARANTEES BLESSINGS OF DUNYA AND AKHERAT.

In verses 3 & 4 of Sura Nooh (71) we learned crucially important principles about 'dealing with Allah' to lead a prosperous life on earth, followed by a fruitful *Akherat*. Hazrat Nooh primarily emphasized on the key qualities of *bandagi* and *Taqwa*, along with obedience of Prophet as the key elements for attaining *Maghferat* and *Rehmat* of Allah. This, essentially, is the core of *Deen* or religion. 'Deen', under the umbrella of Allah's Maghferat and *Rehmat,* provides a comprehensive framework for building humanity's relationship with their Creator, that encompasses every aspect of human existence. Upon unbiased and factual reflection, we shall find *Deen e Islam* as the best system of living, a complete package for life, regarding which Quranic verses provide the most appropriate knowledge and guidance. It is remarkable that, despite this great favour bestowed on humanity, majority is still faltering and misled by the rebellious *shaytan*, resulting in the bitterness of their lives in *Dunya* and ruin of their eternal abode in *Akherat*.

In this segment of our discussion, in the light of initial verses of Sura Nooh (71), we aim to explore how the package of *Deen* unfolds and makes its salient features palpable. Let's study them in detail and in sequence:

a) The initial and most crucial step is to become an *Abd* of Allah. Uttered several times that we refrain from translating an *Abd* as the servant or slave for specific reasons. A servant or a slave is typically restricted in his actions and lacks the freedom to exercise any free will. A slave never enjoys true freedom. In contrast, an *Abd* of Allah embodies the epitome of freedom in the whole of humanity. So, what defines an *Abd*? The one whose self or being is connected to Allah, with Divine inspirations and love flowing unimpeded in their soul. A perfect *Abd* or the perfect human (انسان کامل), maintains and enjoys a superconducting link between his soul and Allah.

The pleasures and peace derived from *bandagi* surpasses all conceivable material pleasures. Although not the main focus of our discussion, interested readers may refer to many prayers by our Imams like *Munajat e Shaaban* taught by Imam Ali (a.s) and *Munajat e Mureedeen* (مناجات مریدین) from Sahifa of Imam Sajjad (a.s) for comprehending the state and status of a true *Abd* of Allah.

b) Upon becoming an *Abd*, the *momin* is blessed with the quality of *Taqwa*. A *Muttaqi* person never forgets Allah, maintaining an awareness or consciousness of His Presence in public and in loneliness. Thus, for an *Abd*, *Taqwa* is not just a trait but his very identity.

c) The next significant component in the package of Deen relates to dealing with the practical aspects of human life such as family, business, and social interactions. A true *Abd* does not rely on personal imagination or discretion to make critical choices and settle for important decisions. Instead, he always adheres to the commands of Allah, by following His Prophet, always placing Islamic teachings and principles above his own desires or whims. Hence, after *Taqwa*, the third dimension of *Deen* is the followership of the Prophet.

d) As a *momin* navigates the ebbs and flows of life, mistakes become inevitable due to inherent human imperfections and unwanted pressures from the society. Thus, emerges the fourth dimension of *Deen* or Godly life which *is Maghferat.* As observed in verses related to the preachings of Hazrat Nooh and will be seen for Hazrat Hud in the next chapter, these great prophets of Allah emphasized repeatedly upon repentance (توبہ) and *Maghferat* (مغفرت). In Sura Nooh, verses 11 & 12 describe the many advantages of *isteghfar* through the statements of Hazrat Nooh. The emphasis on these two pillars of *Deeni* life followed by the Promise of blessings of *Dunya* and *Akherat* can also be appreciated by studying verse 3 of Sura Hud (11). This verse specifically advises our Holy Prophet to seek *Maghferat* of Allah and explain the resulting benefits. The verse is: "And that you seek *maghferat* of your Rab and do *towba* towards Him. He will grant you a beautiful provision (in this life, before death) till an appointed time and will increase the honour of the noble ones. And if you turn away (from this advice), then I fear for you the torment of a formidable day (*Qeyamah*)."

e) As defined earlier, *Maghferat* involves more than just seeking forgiveness after some wrong deed. It entails turning back to Allah wholeheartedly for soul cleansing after recognizing the damages incurred through sins and transgressions. It is similar to the crying appeal of a toddler to his mother once he feels himself troubled by his own filth. Properly sought *Maghferat* also brings the blessing of removing the roots of sinful tendencies from the soul. Removing the "seeds" that could become a cause for sinning is in fact, soul cleansing. This is a brief introduction while in fact, acquiring true *Maghferat* is a complicated process which can be understood in depth by pondering over the discourse # 417 in the third section of Nahj ul Balaghah.

f) A *momin* who remains steadfast on the ways of *Iman*, whose *Towba* towards Allah is accepted (granted Hidayat) and who receives *Maghferat* (cleansing from the effect of sins) is the most blessed person on the earth, alongside *Awlya* and *Masoomeen* (a.s). In this blissful state, the *momin* enjoys the *Barakat* of *Dunya* and *Akherat,* both. This is the matured stage of *Deen* when it begins to yield the intended fruits. Now the momin has entered the domain where he can comprehend and experience the true meaning of human life.

g) The continuity of true blessings (بركات) in *Dunya* is not tied to the accumulation of wealth, indulgence in luxurious food, attainment of lofty ranks or high social status. Rather, it is found in the tranquillity of life energized by a mind focussed on the *bandagi* of Allah and noble deeds. Often, we mistakenly seek the blessings of worldly life in the material things and sensory pleasures. The real blessings of *Dunya* manifest in the noble character that inspires sincere love in the hearts of fellow humans and the lasting positive memories imprinted in their souls after one's departure from this material abode.

2.4. THE OPPORTUNITY TO EMBRACE THE MESSAGE OF ALLAH DOES NOT LAST FOREVER

While examining the verses on catastrophic flood that obliterated the nation of Hazrat Nooh, it's crucial to delve deeper into the spiritual condition of their souls to explore why *Azab* became their inescapable destiny. This analysis is vital not for historical reasons, but to enlighten us on the Divine system that governs human life. It educates us that a nation's prosperity or affliction is fundamentally linked to the condition of human *Nafs*, rather than their external environment and material circumstances. When souls become corrupt and turn away from Allah's message, no force or agency can rescue the nation from ruin and damnation. During the discussion on Hazrat Hud, we shall revisit this issue from a slightly different perspective and notify the causes for *La'nat* and *Azab* on a nation in more detail.

In the last few verses of Sura Nooh, we encounter some distressing sentences as the preaching of Hazrat Nooh continued to fall on deaf ears and hardened hearts. The verses of Sura Nooh (71) began with his *dawah* and continue to the climax where, after 950 years of relentless preaching, Hazrat Nooh could bear no more and pleaded Allah for the eradication of tyrants and the irredeemably corrupt nation. After painful years of preaching, it was evident that their fate—eternal damnation following their demise in the extraordinary deluge—was sealed, underscoring their total spiritual bankruptcy and refusal to embrace even a hint of guidance.

The tragic culmination of the soul-wrenching efforts of an *Ulul Azm* Prophet into a curse for his nation is an undeniable proof of closure of their hearts and shutting down of minds from divine guidance and acceptance of even a speck of *Hidayat*. Their souls were totally impoverished of goodness and corrupted beyond repair. This is the true domain of *La'nat* where every hope of salvation is doomed and no solution exists except banishing from this world and burning into eternal hellfire, as described in the verse 25 of Sura Nooh.

For us, aspiring for a serene and blissful *Akherat* preceded by a virtuous and sin-free worldly life, the stark reminder is to obey Allah's commands while remaining vigilant and watchful over our hearts and minds to ensure spiritual receptivity. It is indeed possible to bodily partake in religious rituals and practices while at the same time, our souls darkening from negligence or rejection of Allah's message.

The desperate pleas of a Prophet for his nation's destruction, due to their complete surrender to evil with no hope for redemption, are both sorrowful and a severe warning. It is heart-wrenching and seriously alarming to read the prayers of a Prophet pleading to Allah to destroy his nation since their hearts were completely taken over by evil and no hope of any recovery was left. We ask Allah for His protection and shelter from such wickedness. We pray for Allah's protection against such malevolence while emphasizing the importance of constantly evaluating our hearts and minds' openness to divine truth.

2.5. CASE OF THE DROWNED SON AND CONDEMNED WIFE

Among the *Ulul Azm* Prophets, Hazrat Nooh endured unparalleled challenges concerning his family. The Quran explicitly mentions that his wife (probably one among a few) and one of his sons were engulfed by the

Azab that annihilated his people. Reflecting on how the immediate family members of an *Ulul Azm* Prophet could be affected by such severe divine retribution is profoundly enlightening. The moral derivatives should be highly instructive for all of us since the Divine principles work the same across all ages in terms of governing and adjudicating human life. The divine decree that applied during Hazrat Nooh's time remain relevant today, emphasizing that there is no evasion from the commandments established by Allah and conveyed by His prophets.

We have already learned about the unfortunate son of Hazrat Nooh in the verses of Sura Hud. It reveals a surprising fact that till the last moment, Hazrat Nooh was unaware of the son's hidden *kufr*. But Quran is amazing when it describes the son's state with a unique phrase. Verse 46 mentions that in response to Hazrat Nooh's query, Allah declared the son as an unchaste deed or an unrighteous act (غير صالح عمل) which is an unusual term since a person is not generally equated to a deed or action. This style of classification illustrates a very important fact. By signifying the drowned son as the embodiment of non-righteousness, Allah explained the reason for his exclusion from the family (اهل) of Hazrat Nooh. The eternal salvation demands proper alignment to the essence of Prophethood, merely having a blood relationship is insufficient. His dissociation from the essence of Prophethood became manifest when he utterly rejected the pleadings of Hazrat Nooh and declared that a mountain would save him from the water (flood). His blindness from seeing the flood as *Azab* also proved his disillusionment from the prophetic message and alignment with detestable deeds of his nation. This event emphasizes that continuously rejecting Allah's message transforms the whole personality of an individual into an indecent or unjust act, perpetually distancing them from acquiring the *Taufeeq* of *towba*.

Besides Hazrat Nooh's son, Quran also informs us in very clear words about the tragic ending of Hazrat Nooh's wife in the final verse of Sura Tehreem (66). These verses utterly and exclusively elucidate that personal relationships never guarantee salvation.

Sura Tehreem (66)

V. 11: And Allah presents the examples for disbelievers (who adopted *kufr* and rejected *Iman*); of the wife of Nooh and the wife of *Lut*. They were under two of Our righteous *Bandegan,* but these women betrayed them and thus, no one could rescue them from Allah (His grip and accountability), and it was ordered to them to enter the hell fire.

The betrayal exhibited by these women, as depicted in the verse, was not of personal nature, but against Prophethood and the mission of preaching Allah's religion. That untrustworthiness was not moral or related to chastity of character. According to some *Riwayat*, these women did not safeguard their husbands' secrets thereby breaching their trust in matters crucial to the Prophetic mission. The importance of faithfulness to the *Wilayah* of Prophets cannot be overstated and any deliberate slackness or perversion in this regard can lead to extremely dire consequences, exemplified by the severe outcomes faced by these two wives of two Prophets.

The events of Hazrat Nooh's drowned son and his condemned wife are powerful reminders for all the *momineen*. They starkly prick our conscience that even those closely related to a grand Prophet are not immune or exempt from Allah's punishment if they leave the path of *Taqwa* and obedience to Allah's message and messenger. These accounts urge believers to introspect: if such close relations of a Prophet can face divine retribution, where do we stand if we disregard the prescribed ways of *Iman* and *Amal e Saleh*? This also reminds us of the inevitability of Allah's Justice on the day of *Qeyamah* when the principles of 'you will reap what you sow' and 'you face nothing but your own attributes (صفات)' will prevail. These Quranic narratives vividly demonstrate the ineffectiveness of attempting to find loopholes or shortcuts to circumvent divine directives, underscoring the vital necessity of following the designated paths of faith and ethical nurturing as we prepare for the Day of *Qeyamah*. These narratives serve as a stern reminder that no one can escape divine scrutiny by devising clever ways to sidestep Allah's laws (قوانين الهى) They compel us to continuously reflect on our own lives: Is it possible to withstand the Day of Judgment by seeking to evade the divine mandates through contrived excuses or searching for the routes alienated from prophetic guidance?

CHAPTER 3
HAZRAT HUD

3.1. INTRODUCTION

Hazrat Hud (a.s) was the first prophet sent towards a powerful and populous nation that flourished in the Middle Easters deserts, succeeding Hazrat Nooh and the great flood. This nation, known as *Aad,* lived, and prospered in the country of *Erum.* Historical research indicates that this was an area situated in the vast desert spewed with dunes and bordered by Yemen, Jordan, and Saudi Arabia. Quran, particularly in verses 6-8 of Sura Fajr (89), highlight their remarkable architectural prowess. Their ability to construct monumental buildings and structures supported by lofty pillars was amazing and unsurpassed, marking them as technological giants of their era. Did their architectural skills and wealth provide them the sustainability they desired? Far from that. Despite their material might, construction skills, and affluence, they could not avert the wrath of Allah once their disobedience to the commands of Allah and rejection of *Hidayat* offered by Prophet Hud made them morally and spiritually corrupt. After several warnings and reprieves, they were ultimately obliterated by a devastating *Azab* that completely demolished their homes and possessions and descended upon them as a fierce storm with unrelenting winds lasting seven days and eight nights.

From the study of verses concerning Hazrat Hud, it can be comprehended that despite their exemplary construction skills, his nation *Aad* was infected with numerous diseases of soul. This fact will be elaborated further as our analysis progresses. Like the nation of Hazrat Nooh, Quran has greatly emphasized the behaviour of chiefs and lords of *Aad* and their arrogant and dismissive responses to the *dawah* of Hazrat Hud.

3.2. STUDY OF QURANIC VERSES ABOUT HAZRAT HUD (A.S)

Our analysis of Quranic verses regarding Hazrat Hud begins with eleventh Quranic sura, named after this eminent Prophet of Allah. Subsequently, we shall enlighten ourselves mainly from the discussion in Sura *Shu'ara* (26) and Sura *Ahqaf* (46), which offer further vital lessons and important guidance to all humanity with reference to the nation of *Aad*.

Let's proceed with the analytical study of Quranic verses.

Sura Hud (11)

V.50: And to the (nation of) *Aad* (We sent) Hud. He said (guided the people), "O my nation! Do *bandagi* of Allah, you have no one worthy of worship (الہ) other than Him. (In your present state) You are nothing but fabricators (of lies against the religion of Allah).

V.51: O my nation! I do not ask you for any reward (since) my reward is on no one except the One Who has founded me [brought me into existence]. Thus, will you not use your intellect?

V. 52: And O my people, seek *Maghferat* of your Rab then return towards Him (*Towba*). He will send down upon you rain in abundance and increase you in strength upon strength, so do not turn away (from Him) as criminals.

In verses of Sura Shu'ara (26) the *dawah* of Hazrat Hud (a.s) is described in more detail encompassing some additional aspects of the Prophetic invitation towards Allah and carving out better and saner humanity. After studying these verses, we shall go into explanation of few noticeable points pertaining to his *dawah* as described in the Quranic verses.

Surah Shu'ara (26)

V. 123: *Aad* denied the Prophets.

V. 124: When their brother Hud said to them why you do not fear (Allah)?

V. 125: "Indeed, I am a trustworthy Prophet for you."

V. 126: "Thus, you observe *Taqwa* of Allah and obey me."

V. 127: "And I do not ask you for any reward, but my reward is upon the Rab of all worlds."

V. 128: "Do you construct upon every high place a monument for your amusement?"

V. 129: "And take for yourself strongholds (huge and strong buildings) as if you are going to live forever on the earth."

V. 130: "And when you seize someone then you seize like tyrants."

V. 131: "Thus, you (must) observe *Taqwa* of Allah and obey me."

V. 132: "And be conscious of Whom who has aided you with what you know."

V. 133: "He has aided you with cattle and children."

V. 134: "And gardens and springs."

V. 135: "Indeed, I fear about you the punishment of a great day."

Let us give a brief explanation of few keywords stated in the verses just enunciated. Later we shall discuss in detail about the prime features of preaching of Hazrat Hud which are permanent in the *dawah* of all prophets.

Explanation:

1. *Taqwa* in many instances in Quran refers to 'Fearing Allah'. This fear is not negative or repulsive. 'To possess or cultivate fear of Allah' means being mindful of the adverse consequences that personal misdeeds and sins can cause. The last two words of the verse 124 (الا تتقون) should translate to 'Why do you not take care to shield yourselves from Allah's wrath (غضب خدا)?'

2. Verse 128 notably highlights Aad's practice of erecting monuments and landmarks at every place that was eye catching or prominent. The word ريع refers to something of higher grade and preferable or it could denote a land at higher elevation so that anything built upon it becomes visible from afar. This and similar verses serve as an extremely important reminder (تذكر), in Quranic morals, about abstaining from ostentation (ريا كارى) which is the foundation of many severe moral diseases like *takabbur* and *hasad*.

3. In verse 130, the Arabic word بطشتم, which means 'you become vicious, or you behave like tyrants', is a very eloquent expression. It serves as a cautionary reminder for all those enjoying commanding authority to exercise kindness and compassion towards their subjects and to treat those they defeat in battle with gentleness. In all worldly interactions, individuals should strive to be kind and lenient towards others, avoiding oppressive behaviour.

DAWAH OF HAZRAT HUD – TYPICAL OF ALL PROPHETS

1. Consistent with the preaching of all Prophets, Hazrat Hud's *dawah* began with advocating for a life free from *shirk*. This fact may seem trivial but according to Quranic teachings, the presence of *shirk* is deemed as a real and the gravest threat to humanity. His *dawah* began with this pivotal guiding sentence: 'Become an *Abd* of Allah besides Whom there is no one worthy or eligible for your worship'. Here, *Abd* refers to a person who establishes a secure and firm connection with Allah. Furthermore, the emphasis on remembering Him as *Ilah* or the one solely worthy of *Ibadat* is a reminder that any person aspiring for a monotheistic (توحیدی) life must safeguard himself from bowing down to different power centres like wealth, authority, and worldly influence.

2. Hazrat Hud invited his nation to embrace Allah as their sole objective in worship and steer clear from fabricating myths and lies in the name of false gods. This issue of self-concoction in the name of religion is as ancient as the religion itself and regrettably, persists in today's modern world, which boasts of its advancements in knowledge, scholarly research, and intellectual excellence.

3. The persuasion to inculcate and practice *Taqwa* is a universal message delivered by every prophet to their nation. It persistently serves as a reminder that true salvation is attainable only through a deep awareness of Allah's Omnipresence (تقوائے الٰہی) and adherence to the conduct of the Prophets (اطاعت رسول اللہ). No one is allowed to interpret the religion based on personal desires or fanciful thoughts.

4. The final sentence of verse 50 in Sura Hud where Hazrat Hud denounced his nation for fabricating lies, reveals that the nation

of *Aad* were practicing some form of worship based on locally invented and self-fantasized notions of a deity or divinity. These beliefs were unfounded and largely the construct of the whims of influential figures, such as priests and rulers, further polluted and distorted by the ignorant interpretations of the general masses. This is another significant aspect of his *dawah* which condemns any fabrication or dealing in lies and promotes only the Truth.

5. Hazrat Hud made it starkly clear that he could not entertain any possibility of accepting material reward or praise or people's appreciation for delivering the message of Allah to His *bandegan*. His expectations were solely from Allah, whom he devotedly served. This tenet echoes across the preachings of all Prophets, as evidenced particularly in the verses of Sura A'raf. All the prophets of Allah unanimously declared to their nations that their endeavours in preaching and guidance were solely for Allah's sake, demanding for nothing from the people other than for them to accept Allah's invitation and abandon their sinful and devious lives. The question then arises: why did Rasool Allah ask for 'Love for the Near ones (مودة فى القربى)' as a return for his preachings? The demand for *Mawaddat* of *Qurba* is for our benefit, not for the Prophet's personal gains. It is akin to a loving father saying to his child, "My best reward in life is that you obey me." Why? "So that you become a noble and honourable person in your life."

6. As observed previously in the *dawah* of Hazrat Nooh, the message of Hazrat Hud similarly underscores the significance of seeking Allah's *Maghferat* as the fundamental agent of evolution and prosperity in this life and *Akherat*. In the discussion section of this chapter, we shall describe in more detail the importance of

repentance and *Isteghfar* (توبہ و استغفار) and its essentiality for the betterment of our lives.

7. Verses 128 & 129 of Sura Shu'ara (26) point out the misuse of the building and construction skills of the nation of *Aad.* Hazrat Hud reprimanded them for their habit of constructing monuments at every prominent location and building their dwellings like fortresses. This reproach was a reminder that in this worldly life, your time on earth is transient, merely a brief duration to be tested in the examination of life. The people who construct grand structures and erect monuments over every place they consider important are driven and inflicted by the belief in their permanence in this world or the notion that their memories are worth preserving. These are fallacious thoughts and discouraged in the religion of Allah. This principle of not investing in the ephemeral is exemplified by Prophets of Allah and Imams, who never constructed luxurious and robust dwellings for themselves. They always embraced a life of contentment and simplicity, fully aware that their eternal abode is somewhere else, and they would certainly leave this world after a brief sojourn.

8. *Dawah* of all Prophets invariably include an aspect of threat or warning of *Azab* for those who persistently reject Allah's message and messenger. In verse 135 of Sura Shu'ara, Hazrat Hud expressed his apprehension (خوف) for Azab of a tremendous day to befall *Aad,* without specifying whether it pertains to the *Azab* of this *Dunya* or the *Azab* of *Akherat?* However, the implication is clear that for a nation destined for *Azab,* the hellfire is waiting for them in *Akherat,* while their worldly life becomes deprived of every goodness and prosperity. Most likely, by the great and tremendous day (*Youm e*

Azeem), Hazrat Hud actually meant that fateful day when the nation of *Aad* experienced the wrath of Allah, and their traces were obliterated from the face of this world.

ARGUMENTS OF HAZRAT HUD WITH HIS NATION

The *dawah* of Hazrat Hud was logical and inspiring. However, as observable in the case of every Prophet, the chiefs, lords, and materially powerful from his nation immediately jumped into confrontation. This dynamical situation can be assessed in the following verses of Sura Hud (11), describing the argumentation of Hazrat Hud and his nation in detail:

Sura Hud (11):

V. 53: They (powerful from his nation) replied, "O Hud, you have not come to us with clear proof, and we shall not abandon our gods upon your word, nor will we believe in you."

V. 54: [In reply they expressed their skepticism about Hazrat Hud as:] "And we can conclude that some of our gods have possessed you with evil." He (Hud) replied, "Certainly I call Allah as (my) witness, and you too become witness that I am completely dissociated from what you commit as shirk."

V.55: "(and from) those whom you associate (with Allah) apart from Him. Thus, you unleash all your schemes against me and do not give me any reprieve."

V. 56: "Surely, I trust in Allah (توكل على الله) Who is my Rab and your Rab. There is not a single creature moving (on earth) except under His complete control. Indeed, my Rab is on *the firm and straight highway* (صراط مستقيم). [The Arabic translation of *sirat*(صراط) is the pathway, which is broad, free of turns and twists, and carries the people upon it straight to their destination, that's why I have translated *sirat* as the highway.]

V.57: (Hazrat Hud further admonished them), "But if you turn away (in rebellion), I have already delivered to you what I have been sent with. (Your rejection of the message of Allah will not bear any fruit for you) since my Rab will soon (displace you from this comfort and luxury) and replace you with another nation while you could not harm Him in the least. Indeed, my Rab is absolutely vigilant over everything."

Explanation:

a) Similar to Hazrat Nooh, Hazrat Hud encountered responses that were naïve and devoid of any true understanding, characterized more by wrangling and disputation rather than a genuine willingness to learn what was not previously known or lucid. Through these arguments, we can realize the level of ignorance of Hazrat Hud's nation and to what extent they had wrapped themselves in the veils of self-deception. Their declaration regarding Hazrat Hud, as mentioned in verse 54 is a stark reminder of their travesty when they considered Hazrat Hud to be possessed by some demonic god of theirs. It reveals that besides worshipping multiple gods they also believed in the influence of demonic malevolent deities capable of corrupting people's souls and leading them to lose their reason and intelligence. It is an inescapable fact that after passing of thousands of years such baseless beliefs are still haunting many sections and societies across the human race. Truth can never prevail unless these unfounded, self-perceived, and fabricated lies are banished.

b) Hazrat Hud unequivocally rejected any claims of demonic possession and sought protection in the Power of Allah from all forms of ignorance and perversion. Like all Prophets, he exhibited complete indifference regarding the schemes and plotting of his enemies, instead invited them to bring forth whatever they could to eliminate him and his *dawah*. His unflinching stance exemplifies the resilience and unwavering commitment of Prophethood to the divine responsibilities, regardless of the ferocity of opposition.

c) In verse 56, Hazrat Hud presents a compelling and powerful reason to have staunch faith and complete trust in Allah, by elaborating that Allah is on *Sirat e Mustaqeem*. *Sirat e Mustaqeem* symbolizes absolute truth and complete absence of any evil presence or influence. This purity is a proof of His complete authority over the lives and destinies of every creature walking on the face of the earth. So, if He possesses all-encompassing and indisputable control over every life and existence then who else could we turn to for resolution in times of trouble, support during adversity, and for triumph over our enemies?

THE CURSED STATE OF A NATION BEFORE THE ARRIVAL OF AZAB

Verses 136 to 139 in Sura Shu'ara (26) depict a peculiar behaviour exhibited by *Aad* and characterize those who become deserving of the *Azab* of Allah. This behaviour is their descent into the abyss of absolute denial and their shift towards outright rejection of divine guidance. This transition to stubborn refusal of Hazrat Hud can be attributed to their hearts and minds becoming sealed off from the Divine Light!

With the help of few verses from Sura Shu'ara (26), we shall now analyse the typically cursed state of the nation of *Aad*, the degradation of their souls and minds as exhibited in their behaviour before the arrival of *Azab*.

Sura Shu'ara (26)

V. 136: They flatly told Hazrat Hud, "It makes no difference for us whether you advise (us), or you cease to be among the advisors."

V. 137: "It is nothing but the conduct or behaviour of those who have already passed (before us)."

V. 138: "And we are not to be the ones who are punished."

V. 139: Thus, they denied and hence We destroyed them. Indeed, in that (the events of Aad) there is a sign and most of them were never among the believers.

The hardening of hearts as demonstrated in their vows and assertions described in verse 136 of Sura Shu'ara was a clear sign of the ultimate *Azab* lurking in their proximity. This fact is extremely mind-provoking and alarming that the minds and intellect of those in the vicinity of *Azab* become closed and their brazen shamelessness before the representative of Allah keeps on increasing. It is very instructive to study the arrogant and haughty stance of *Aad* against Hazrat Hud which consists of the following main features:

a) **Total Dismissal:** Their initial standpoint was a total rejection of Hazrat Hud, refusing even to consider his counsel. A complete closure of minds!

b) **Indifference to Precedents:** Then they further tried to justify their stance by asserting that, like Hazrat Hud, there were others in earlier generations as well, who tried to prevent their communities from living their preferred life and motivated them to obey Allah, but such people and their stories bear 'no significance or impact on us'.

c) **Disregard for Divine Retribution**: Lastly, they dismissed the possibility of any *Azab* that could grab them, a denial that eventually destroyed them. This extremely perilous attitude cautions us about a very destructive mindset, i.e., during the period of affluence, *shaytan* disillusions people into believing that their material wealth is eternal, and they are immune to loss or divine accountability irrespective of what they do and how they behave.

Ultimately the recalcitrance and obduracy of the nation of Aad resulted in their ruination; their lofty cities effaced from the face of this earth as if they had never existed. This obliteration underscores the transient nature of worldly power and the futility of arrogance against Divine Will. Merely their stories are remaining for others' morals and learning important lessons of life. No tears were shed for them, nor did their memories exist in any heart. فاعتبروا يا اولى الابصار .

DESCENDING OF AZAB AND ULTIMATE DESTRUCTION

We shall continue with the verses of Sura Hud (11) to which we shall combine a few verses from Sura Qamar (54) and Sura Ahqaf (46) and conclude the description of the prophetic life of Hazrat Hud which terminates with the Divine wrath falling on his nation owing to their persistent disbelief and defiance.

Sura Hud (11)

V.58: And when Our order (امر) came, We rescued (to safety) Hud and those who accepted *Iman* with him by our *Rehmat*. And we liberated (spared) them (the momineen) from a harsh and inescapable *Azab*.

V.59: That was (the nation of) *Aad*. They denied (and rejected) the signs of their Rab and dissuaded from the path of His messengers and followed the command of every rebellious tyrant.

V. 60: They were followed by a curse (لعنت) in this Dunya and also on the day of *Qeyamah*. Beware, surely *Aad* denied their Rab and take heed that *Aad* the nation of Hud (were) shunned off.

The descendance of *Azab* upon the nation of *Aad* is also described in some other surahs. For instance, these verses of Sura Qamar (54) succinctly but lucidly describe the form of Azab that brought their terminal end.

Sura Qamar (54)

V. 18: *Aad* vehemently rejected (the messenger of Allah and His message) hence, (observe) how was my *Azab* and the warning.

V.19: Indeed, We send upon them a furious wind on a day of unending misery.

V.20: (that storm) snatched and smashed the people and left them (devoid of all life) like uprooted trunks of date palm trees.

Some further enlightening aspects and profound insight can be found in the verses of Sura Ahqaf (46) which highlight the complete ignorance (غفلت) of the people of *Aad* as they faced their impending doom.

Sura Ahqaf (46)

V. 24: Then when they (*Aad*) saw the (*Azab* in the form of dense clouds) approaching their valleys, they said (in joy), "This is a cloud bringing us rain." "Nay, it is what you were hastening for, a storm in which there is a painful punishment."

V.25: It demolished everything (in its way) by the command (امر) of its Rab. (And therefore, once it passed over their cities) nothing was visible except their dwellings (in ruins). That's how we recompense the criminal nations.

Generally, reward or recompense (جزا) is used in a positive sense but in some cases like here, it is meant as a repayment of the consequences of evil deeds.

These verses illustrate the inability of *Aad* to recognize the warning signs of their approaching destruction and highlight a grave level of ignorance and spiritual blindness. This tragic misperception, where the very *Azab* sent as a consequence of their denial and misdeeds was mistaken for a blessing, underscores the depth of their delusion and estrangement from divine understanding.

3.3. REASONS FOR BEFALLING OF CURSE OR *LA'NAT* OF ALLAH ON A NATION OR GROUP OF PEOPLE

If we carefully look at the verses describing the wrath of Allah and *La'nat* befalling the nation of *Aad*, a few core principles could be identified and presented as the derived morals. There are three reasons given in verse 59 of Sura Hud (11) for *La'nat* to befall the nation of *Aad* which are:

i. They denied and rejected the message and *Deen* of their Rab, delivered to them through His Prophet with clear signs and without any ambiguity. It must be realised that in the absence of physical presence of Allah's representative, there might be some allowance for not truly acknowledging and obeying the true message of the Almighty. However, in case of *Deen* presented and articulated by a Prophet himself, following rejection there is no escape from the *Azab* and destruction. In our current era, without the physical presence of the Twelfth Imam (a.s), we face a significant disadvantage. Yet, this also acts as an indirect blessing, for despite our numerous flaws and deviations from the prescribed ways of Islam, we are spared from immediate and outright destruction. Such a reprieve was not available to *Aad*, who had a *Masoom* Prophet among them, directly delivering Allah's message.

ii. The second grave issue, which incurred *La'nat* upon them, was their insistence on deviating from or failure to adhere to the *seerah* (conduct) of the Prophets. It must be carefully noted that in verse 59, when Allah talks about their deviation and disobedience (معصیت) the object of the sentence is 'Prophets (plural)', not only their Prophet who was Hazrat Hud. This choice of words emphasizes that the path and teachings of all Prophets of Allah are unified, and to deny one Prophet is to reject them all. Why does this deviation bring *La'nat* upon a nation? Because there exists only one path in life that is *Noor* and salvation which is the *seerah* or lifestyle of Prophets. All other paths lead to doom and darkness (ظلمت) ultimately culminating in *La'nat* and *Azab*.

iii. The third reason, which effectively follows from the preceding one, involves their allegiance and obedience to the commands and wishes of every tyrant who adamantly opposed and rejected the message of Allah. These tyrants were the influential and resourceful people of their nation who considered *Deen* as their major adversary, believing it to be a threat that could diminish their material might. Once *Aad* deserted the ways of Prophets, they were captured and subjugated by the despots of their time. This propensity and penchant for the path laid down by the enemies of Allah and His Prophets represents an issue of grave importance that is critically overlooked while searching for the causes of *La'nat* befalling a nation. Typically, we attribute various moral sins and transgressions as the triggering cause of *Azab*, but often overlook yielding to the tyrants (طاغوت) and aligning with the enemies of Allah as a leading factor in a nation's downfall. This matter is so serious in the Divine rule book that even an inclination towards the adversaries of Allah warrants severe eternal punishment, commencing from the moment one departs this *Dunya* and enters the realm of *barzakh* (برزخ). This extremely fearful fate can be observed in these verses of **Sura Mohammad (47)**:

V. 25: Indeed, those who turned back [returned to كفر] after the true guidance (هدايت) was made clear to them; (it is) the *shaytan* who tempted them and lured them with (false) hopes.

V. 26: [Why *shaytan* got better of them despite being Muslims, apparently?] That is because they covertly assured those who detested what Allah has sent (as *Wahi*) and pledged, "We shall obey you in certain matters." And (irrespective of their secrecy) Allah knows their innermost secrets.

V. 27: So, what will be the state when the angels extract their souls (from their bodies) while hitting their faces and backs? [Notably, this verse is describing the fate of those Muslims who conspire against Prophet and make allegiance with the enemies of the revelation of Allah.]

V.28: That is because they (the sufferers of *Azab*) pursued whatever Allah despised and hated whatever pleased Him, thus, He made their deeds futile (worthless as if nothing).

3.4. THE DENIAL OF TRUTH RENDERS THE FACULTIES OF LISTENING AND OBSERVING FUTILE

In verse 26 of **Sura Ahqaf (46)** Allah expresses His sorrow over the unfortunate fate of *Aad*, highlighting that despite being endowed with the precious gifts of hearing and sight (سمع و بصر) —faculties meant for listening, reflecting, and observing—these gifts were squandered by that nation. *Aad* made good use of these Divine gifts in their *Dunya* but utterly disregarded them in the matters of *Akherat* or eternal life! The verse is as follows:

Sura Ahqaf (46)

V.26: And surely, We had established them (*Aad*) in the earth unlike how We have settled you (O Meccans or the people of *Quraysh*). And (in addition to material affluence) We had gifted them with (the faculties of) listening and sight and (blessed them with) heart and intellect (سمع، بصر اور فوءاد), but neither their listening nor sight and observing, nor intellect could fetch them any benefit when they persisted in denial of the signs (and message) of Allah. Consequently, they were overwhelmed by the very thing they were in habit of ridiculing.

The stage where listening and observing becomes ineffective and intellect is rendered futile marks an extremely critical and concerning juncture in the lives of both individuals and the nations. From this verse, it becomes evident that people can be smart, skilful, and knowledgeable in their worldly affairs yet remain ignorant and engulfed in total darkness regarding the matters of their *Akherat*. Why this seemingly counter-intuitive but alarmingly probable scenario is encountered by many people or nations, one example of which is the nation of *Aad*? Upon careful examination of the words of verse 26, it will be revealed that this plight befell the nation of *Aad* due to their denial or outright rejection of the signs or (آیات) of Allah.

Q. What are the "Signs of Allah", denial of which bring such horrible retributions?

A: Sign of Allah (آیات الہی) refers to every phenomenon and aspect of creation that mirrors and reveals an Attribute of Allah, guiding creatures towards the Creator. Under this definition, we come to realize that the whole complex of life, the universe, and human beings themselves exist as the Sign of Allah. These Signs manifest Allah's Creative Powers evident in everything and everyone. Moreover, the Scriptures and Revelations of Allah communicated through His Prophets and preserved as compiled texts and documents, also constitute a very important segment of Signs of Allah. For the nation of Aad, Hazrat Hud and his *dawah* were the clearest sign of Allah.

Q. Why the denial of Allah's Signs seal the hearts and minds?

A: Allah has endowed humans with the invaluable gifts of sight, hearing, and intellect, enabling them to perceive, absorb and embrace the omnipresent Signs of Allah and submit to Him as an *Abd*. This submission cultivates a personal relationship with the Creator, fostering humility and devotion, and empowering individuals to make positive contributions to the world and become a source of blessings for other beings and the environment. However, the tragic reality is that majority of individuals and nations choose to pursue exactly the opposite path and employ their faculties of perception and reasoning to serve their lusts and fulfill their sinister motives and nefarious goals, resulting in closure of these faculties. Closure or shutting off means that neither *Hidayat* can be received through eyes and ears nor hearts are capable any more of absorbing the Divine Light.

The narration of *Aad*, as recounted in the Quran, serves as a vivid illustration of those who preferred spiritual blindness over soul enlightenment. Those people ignored the divine messages conveyed through their senses and shut themselves off from the wisdom accessible through intellect. Quran also informs us that this disregard for divine guidance and misuse of human faculties, as seen in ancient civilizations like Aad and *Thamud*, is a recurring theme throughout human history. For instance, in this verse of Sura A'raf (7), Quran regards such people as inferior to grazing cattle, not metaphorically but in actuality; a fact that will become glaringly evident in the domain of Truth (*Qeyamah*).

Sura A'raf (7)

V. 179: And indeed, We have destined many among Jinn and Humans for Hell. (Why?) They have hearts (faculties of thinking and reasoning) but do not go into the depths [they fail to use the faculty of thinking and reasoning to grasp truth and reality] and for them, there are eyes but do not see with them (no vision and observation) and they have ears but no listening with them. They are like cattle, in fact, much lower in stature (than these animals). [Despite being endowed with these precious faculties, they behave and live like grazing cattle, only interested in satisfying their lusts and hunger.] They are heedless (their souls in a deep state of ignorance and slumber).

3.5. MATERIAL AFFLUENCE AND TECHNOLOGICAL EXCELLENCE ARE NO ASSURANCE FOR SAFETY AGAINST *AZAB* OF ALLAH

Despite belonging to antiquity, the nation of *Aad* is mentioned in Quran as the builders of unique cities and mighty structures as can be observed in the following verses of **Sura Fajr (89)**:

V. 6: Have you not seen how your Rab dealt with *Aad* ?

V. 7: (Inhabitants of) *Eram* possessors of lofty pillars.

V. 8: And among the cities no one built up like theirs'.

These small verses eloquently describe that *Aad* were the people who built grand structures upon high and lofty pillars. Verse 8 specifically highlights *Aad's* unparalleled construction and architectural prowess among nations, with Quran notifying that no city has since matched their distinctive features. This serves as a testament to their technological brilliance. However, when combined with verses 21 to 28 of Sura *Ahqaf* (46) the fact becomes undeniable that *Aad* simultaneously exhibited extreme delinquency towards the message and messenger of Allah. Driven by their wealth and influence, they deemed sinful behaviour and tyranny permissible. Keen on immortalizing their memories and presence in this world, they erected monuments wherever they saw an elevated terrain. Despite their wishes and efforts, they could not evade divine wrath, and their grand structures and monuments ultimately met their demise, buried forever somewhere beneath the desert sands. *Rab* of worlds is neither oblivious nor could be deceived by the ways of evil, as we found a bit later in verses of Sura Fajr (89):

V.11: These nations *(Aad, Thamud* and *Firon)* transgressed throughout the cities.

V.12: spreading corruption (فساد) in abundance.

V.13: Thus, your Rab unleashed on them a lash of *Azab*

V.14: Indeed, Your Rab is truly vigilant (upon these tyrants).

The ineffectiveness of wealth in guaranteeing protection and a prosperous future, is also described in the example of *Qaroon*. Verses 76-82 of **Sura Qasas (28)** discuss his mindset, magnitude of his opulence and its eventual annihilation. Most noticeable is verse 77, which offers a universal and invaluable advice to everyone who enjoys material wealth. Let's have a brief review:

V.77: Seek the home of *Akherat* (Eternal Blessings) by means of what Allah has granted you (from wealth and resources in this world) while not forgetting your share from *Dunya*; and behave beautifully (to others) as Allah has been beautiful to you, and do not seek to spread corruption in the land. Certainly, Allah does not like those who cause corruption.

People such as the nation of *Aad* and individuals like *Qaroon*, must understand the importance of living in the hearts and minds of future generations if they wish their memories to be preserved in this world. That is what constitutes a man's noble share from this worldly life (نصيب دنيا). Allah explicitly states in verse 96 **Sura Maryam (19)** that He instils genuine love in the hearts of people for those *momineen* who perform noble deeds. This sincere adoration and deep respect are the most enduring memories and lasting legacies an individual or a nation can achieve in this world. Considering a small life spanning 60 or 70 years, loving memories can last for centuries, as witnessed in the continuing legacies of Prophets and saints (اولیاء الہی).

The narratives from the Quran clarify beyond doubt the essential conditions for the thriving of any nation, highlighting that true prosperity is not linked to material wealth, nor is it dependent on constructing grand monuments, lofty buildings, and luxurious palaces. The real secret to evading divine punishment and obliteration lies in *bandagi* of the Almighty and obeying His Prophets. Mind you, no harm in practicing science and technology; when combined with *bandagi*, these endeavours transform into blessings upon blessings, enriching both the spiritual and material dimensions of life. (نور علی نور)

CHAPTER 4
HAZRAT SALEH

4.1. INTRODUCTION

Hazrat Saleh (a.s) was another eminent pre-Abrahamic Prophet, sent after Hazrat Nooh and Hud to the nation of *Thamud* who also lived in the Arabian land. Perhaps their abode was in the vicinity of the city '*Madaen e saleh*' situated in modern-day Saudi Arabia. Like the nation of *Aad* their construction and building skills were exceptional. In many surahs of *Quran e Majeed*, we find the description of Hazrat Saleh and his confrontation with the people of *Thamud*. They were among those few nations who faced Divine retribution through a severe punishment—a massive and intense scream—that led to their annihilation.

Thamud too, was corrupted by sins and stigmas of ignoble character. Allah sent Hazrat Saleh to this nation for *Hidayat* and reformation. He was immediately confronted by some (not the majority) influential people who were ruling over the nation of *Thamud,* and apparently enjoying complete dominance over their people. They demanded a unique miracle from Hazrat Saleh as a proof of his Prophethood. Their wish was fulfilled when a she-camel with her baby miraculously emerged from a mountain. But the fulfilment of demand came at a price. The she-camel used to drink all the water from the water source used daily by *Thamud* thus, leaving behind city dwellers thirsty and searching for water. This situation created a tense environment for Hazrat Saleh while dealing with his nation. Hazrat Saleh proposed a solution that the camel and the people should have their separate turns of fetching and using water on alternate days. This arrangement carried on for a short duration, but the evil-minded people in the nation of Hazrat Saleh could not accept this peace and one of them cut off the legs of she-camel. Unable to walk and badly injured, the camel gradually met her death.

Following this barbaric act, Hazrat Saleh declared the advent of Divine punishment or *Azab* on the nation of *Thamud*. If we consult the *Ahadith* of Masoomeen (a.s) in this regard, we come to know that even after this heinous crime Allah waited for *Thamud* to repent, but like *Aad* their hearts were hardened and blackened by sinning and revolting against Allah. The perdition eventually arrived as an immensely loud and intense banging sound that pierced their brains and the *kafereen* turned into corpses while sitting in their fortress-like residences. Hazrat Saleh and the *momineen* with him were spared of this *Azab*.

The prophetic life of Hazrat Saleh shares many similarities with those of Hazrat Nooh and Hazrat Hud (a.s), highlighting that, despite differences in locations and times, the essence of Prophethood remains consistent. Therefore, the discussion on Hazrat Saleh should be viewed as a continuation of the analyses on the lives of the two prophets mentioned in the previous chapters. There are some differences, such as the occurrence of a miracle at the insistence of the people and the downfall of the entire nation due to presence and actions of a few malicious individuals. However, the central themes of *Bandagi, Taqwa* and obedience to Allah's Prophet are the recurring themes in this narrative as well.

4.2. DISCUSSION ON HAZRAT SALEH (A.S) IN THE LIGHT OF QURANIC VERSES

We shall explore and discuss the life of Hazrat Saleh by drawing lessons from four different Surahs. Similar to the approach taken in the previous two chapters, we aim to extract key lessons through an analysis of Quranic verses. Our journey begins with Surah Shu'ara (26), which offers a comprehensive account of Hazrat Saleh's prophetic life from its beginning to its end.

Surah Shu'ara (26)

V. 141: *Thamud* denied the Prophets.

V. 142: When their brother Saleh said to them why you do not fear (Allah).

V. 143: Indeed, I am a trustworthy Prophet for you.

V. 144: Thus, you fear Allah (practice *Taqwa*) and obey me.

V. 145: And I do not ask from you any reward, but my reward is upon the Rab of all worlds.

V. 146: Will you be left in what is here safe and secure (forever)?

V. 147: In gardens and springs.

V. 148: In agricultural fields and date palms.

V. 149: And (in) what you carve from the mountains; homes with great skill.

V. 150: Thus, you fear Allah (observe *Taqwa*) and obey me.

V. 151: And do not follow the commands of transgressors.

V. 152: Those who spread corruption in the earth and do not create goodness.

V. 153: They said indeed you are among the bewitched (i.e., under the negative influence of some magic).

V. 154: You are nothing but a human like us, hence [we do not care about you], (you may) bring forth any sign (punishment) if you are among the truthful.

Explanation:

1. *Thamud* was the name of the nation to which Hazrat Saleh was sent. The primary or main characteristic attributed to them in these verses is their denials of Allah's Message and their aversion to the *dawah* of the Prophet (Hazrat Saleh) sent towards them.

2. From the description in Sura Shu'ara (26), it has become clear that like *Aad*, *Thamud* was a powerful and organized but arrogant and sinful nation. They were not prepared to realize the vast array of blessings of Allah upon their nation and follow the path of thankfulness (*Shukr*).

3. In the Quran, Hazrat Saleh is referred to as a brother of the nation of *Thamud*, as seen in verse 142. This emphasizes the notion that a Prophet engages with his nation with the care and love of a brother. The mentioning of brotherly love signifies that the role of a Prophet extends beyond merely teaching or educating the people; it involves making sacrifices and enduring hardships to enhance the quality and blessings of their lives in this world (*Dunya*) and in the hereafter (*Akherat*).

4. Verse 145, where Hazrat Saleh declared his disinterest in any reward for his efforts to convey Allah's message, echoes the sentiments previously expressed by Hazrat Nooh and Hazrat Hud to their respective peoples. This uniformity of purity and sincerity among all prophets, despite the vast temporal gaps between their lifetimes, underscores a fundamental principle of prophethood: Prophets are not driven by personal motives or the pursuit of worldly benefits in their preaching; they are solely dedicated to disseminating Allah's commands and guidance according to His Will.

5. This stance also emphasizes the timeless and unchanging nature of the truth delivered by the prophets. Despite the centuries that may separate their earthly existences, the core of their teachings remains consistent, rooted in the principles of *Iman*, accountability, and *Bandagi* of Allah. This consistency across different eras and cultures is a testament to the universal and eternal truth of their message, aiming to lead humanity towards a path of spiritual enlightenment and moral integrity.

6. The verses (146 – 149) imply that *Thamud's* country was exceedingly fertile, blessed with abundant resources by Allah. In addition, they were skilful people, capable of building strong and robust structures by carving into the hard rocks. In Sura Fajr (89) we also find the information that *Thamud* excelled in carving rocky mountains to establish their residential places and other "buildings" for various purposes. Despite these blessings, their faith in Allah and acknowledgment of His inescapable accountability were non-existent. Instead of attributing their prosperity and abilities to divine Grace, their belief system - shaped by their lords and worldly masters - misled them into believing that their material success was eternal

and self-sustained. This false conviction allured and led them down a path of sin, worshipping false gods, and tyrannical oppression.

7. By verse 150, the advice about observing *Taqwa* and obeying the Prophet is reiterated for the third time, underscoring the significance of these virtues at the level and scale of the whole society. As observed in the discussions on Hazrat Nooh and Hud, these directives are not limited to a particular nation or group of people; they are a universal call to all nations—past, present, and future—to adopt God-consciousness (*Taqwa*) and adhere to the values and actions (*seerah*) exhibited in the lives of Allah's Prophets. Without these foundations, their material wealth will prove futile and incapable of shielding them from Allah's displeasure.

8. Hazrat Saleh, akin to his predecessors, encountered opposition and rejection, primarily from the chiefs and the influential members of the Thamud. A couple of verses from **Surah Al-Mu'minun (23)**, mentioned below, capture their statements, and reveal a common strategy employed by the opponents of divine messengers. They always sought to undermine the Prophets by focusing on their human attributes, insinuating that their humanity somehow diminishes the credibility of their divine message:

V.33: And the chiefs from his (Hazrat Saleh's) nation - who denied (his *dawah*) and rejected the meeting of judgment day and were extravagant wasters in the life of Dunya - declared, "he is nothing but a common person like you, he eats from the food and drinks what you drink from."

V.34: "And if you obey a person like yourself then certainly you will become losers (will not attain any benefit in life)."

This line of arguments reflects a deep irony and was nothing but a deceptive trap for the people. The chiefs, who were themselves human, coerced people into obeying their commands, without considering their own humanity as an obstruction to obedience; yet they shamelessly dismissed the Prophet's call towards Allah on the grounds of his human existence. This hypocrisy reveals their manipulation and self-serving motives, aiming to maintain their power and control, while undermining the spiritual and moral guidance offered by the Prophet.

FIRST MIRACLE IN THE PROPHETIC HISTORY

In the Prophetic life of Hazrat Saleh, the conflict took an unprecedented turn compared to the events involving earlier Prophets. The novel phenomenon was the demand for a miracle; to exhibit something extraordinary, far beyond the power and capacity of every human being. Verse 154 of **Sura Shu'ara (26)** concluded that Hazrat Saleh was challenged to present a definitive sign to affirm his Prophethood. With Allah's permission, Hazrat Saleh responded to this demand by manifesting a miracle, the details, and consequences of which are further explored in the subsequent verses of Sura Shu'ara.

V. 155: He (Hazrat Saleh) said, "This is a she-camel (as the sign from Allah); for her, there is a share for drink, and for you is a share on a given day.

V. 156: And do not touch her with harm so that you may be seized by the punishment of a great day.

V. 157: Then they cut her legs and ended up being regretful.

V. 158: Thus, the punishment got hold of them (and brought upon them complete destruction). Indeed, in that there is a sign and most of them have been unbelievers.

Verses from Surah Al-Qamar (54) also delve into the issues surrounding the appearance of the she-camel as a miraculous sign from Allah. Let's examine these three verses from **Sura Qamar (54)** where we discover a crucial insight that the camel was not merely sent to fulfill their wish or demand but was actually intended as a test or trial for the *Thamud*:

V.27: Surely, We are sending a she-camel as a 'test' (فتنة) for them, so (O Saleh) be watchful on them and have patience.

V.28: And make them aware that the water must be divided (shared) between them and her, each of them showing up at his respective turn (on alternate days).

V.29: (Instead of obeying this advice) they incited their companion who then dared to cut her legs (and killed her)

Explanation:

1. After launching scathing attacks on the personality of a Hazrat Saleh, these tyrants proceeded to their next tactic, which involved demanding the miraculous appearance of a camel from a mountain. Such urgings to bring out some extraordinary signs or events as the proof of Prophethood were nothing but a disgusting attempt to undermine Prophet's status in the eyes of people. The tyrants expect that the Prophet would be unable to fulfill these abnormal demands. This practice of asking for miracles happened to many Prophets and Allah often responded to their demands, and miracles occurred, as we observe in the case of Hazrat Saleh. Yet, these foolish and

arrogant people failed to realize that now they are flirting with a grave danger. After manifestation of a clear sign, refusal to accept the divine message and persistent defiance against the Prophet invariably leads to *Azab* and destruction.

2. Following the repeated demands of the chiefs from *Thamud*, Allah 'created' a huge she-camel (ناقة) and her offspring from a mountain as a testament to the truthfulness of Hazrat Saleh. This miracle held profound significance because the people of this nation, highly skilled in carving dwellings inside mountains, witnessed a living creature emerge from those very mountains, a marvel brought forth by their Prophet's prayer. As master craftsmen they were in a great position to comprehend the nature of miracle manifested to them. Had there been any semblance of justice in their souls, their heads would have bowed down in submission. Alas! That did not happen, and these people remained stubborn against Hazrat Saleh and kept on marching the ways of perdition.

3. The camel was a source of examination and hence it threw the people into a novel difficulty. Her size and needs were so enormous that she drank the entirety of the lake's water - the main source of water for the people - in a single day. This unpleasant situation greatly frustrated the people of *Thamud*. To resolve the dispute, Hazrat Saleh decreed that one day should be reserved for the camel and the next dedicated to the people to draw water from the source.

4. Hazrat Saleh, afraid of the potential harm these wicked people might inflict upon the she-camel, explicitly warned them about the threat of *Azab* if they attempt to hurt or injure the animal. In verse 156,

we find Hazrat Saleh issuing the warning to his nation for being very careful about any malevolence towards the sign of Allah.

5. The wicked miserably failed to learn any lesson and one of them gruesomely cut off the legs of she-camel, resulting in her death. That was the last nail in their coffin and shortly thereafter, the entire nation of Thamud, despite their material might, was obliterated from earthly existence.

DESCENT OF 'AZAB' FOR DISRESPECTING THE MIRACLE

The verses presented thus far, and the ensuing discussion indubitably enlighten us that once *Thamud's* plea for a distinguished sign of Allah's Authority and His Prophet's truthfulness was fulfilled through a miracle, their nation edged a step closer to the *Azab*! This statement may seem strange, but the principle is irrefutable: 'as signs of Allah become increasingly evident, the window of rejecting the divine message gets narrower.' Demanding a miracle is not like ordering a cuisine, the affairs may become terribly unpleasant if the miracle is disrespected or maltreated. This is precisely what happened to *Thamud*. The appearance of the she-camel was a clear manifestation of Allah's power, a sign meant to guide them towards *Iman* and obedience. However, by plotting against and ultimately killing the she-camel, *Thamud* crossed the red line from verbal scepticism into outright defiance and disrespect of Allah's sign. This act of shameless defiance did not just signify their rejection of the *dawah* of Hazrat Saleh; it was a direct challenge to Allah's Authority.

Another factor worth considering in the episode of *Thamud* is the presence of a small, elite group that played a pivotal role in shaping the nation's response to the Prophetic message. This group, characterized by their power, cunning, influence, and malicious intentions, managed to steer the public response against Hazrat Saleh, despite the clear signs and teachings he brought from Allah. The Quranic verses in **Sura Naml (27)** and **Sura Shams (91)** shed light on this aspect, illustrating how this dominant faction's influence led to tragic consequences. Sadly enough, the people did not resist or even oppose their directives, eventually leading that elite group to become the main cause and prime reason for the destruction of the nation of *Thamud*.

We shall begin with **Sura Naml (27)** and then add verses of **Sura Shams (91)** to deepen our analysis.

Sura Namal (27)

V. 45: And We sent towards *Thamud* their brother Saleh (who said to them), "Do *bandagi* of Allah." Then they became two quarrelling groups.

V. 46: Saleh pleaded to them, "O my nation, why do you hasten to seek the evil (eternal punishment) before goodness (prosperity and salvation by obeying Allah)? Don't you seek *Maghferat* of Allah in the hope that you may be granted (His) *Rehmat?*"

V.47: They replied, "You and your followers are a bad omen for us." Saleh answered, "Your omens are in the presence of Allah, (nay) but you are a people subjected to *fitnah* (test and trial)."

V.48: And in the city, a group of **nine men** were the instigators (and perpetrators) and responsible for spreading corruption in the land and they were not (among those) who set things right.

V. 49: They vowed, "Let us swear by Allah that we shall attack him (Saleh) and his family in the (darkness) of night and then (after killing them) will say to his heirs, 'We did not witness (or have any knowledge) about the killing of his family and surely we are telling the truth.'"

V.50: And they planned their schemes, and We (Allah) planned (too) while they were (totally) unaware (of My plan).

V. 51: Thus, have a look at the result (and consequences) of their planning. We utterly demolished them (the planners) and their nation, all together.

V. 52: So, those are their homes, abandoned and ruined because of their injustice and wrongdoing (ظلم). Indeed, in that (episode of *Thamud*) there is a sign for the people of knowledge.

Sura Shams (91)

V. 11: *Thamud* thoroughly rejected (the message of Allah) out of rebellion and arrogance.

V. 12: When the most wicked of them stood up (and came forward to kill the she-camel who had emerged as a miracle.)

V. 13: Then warned them, the messenger of Allah, "(Beware of) the camel of Allah and her turn to drink."

V. 14: But they denied him and slaughtered her (the she-camel), thus, their Rab crushed them due to their sins and levelled it.

V. 15: And He has no fear of any repercussion.

Explanation:

1. Verse 47 of Sura Naml (27) highlights the *Thamud*'s dismissal of Hazrat Saleh's Prophethood as an unwelcome or negative omen, drawing a parallel to the attitudes of *Aad* against Hazrat Hud. This

reflects a common pattern of indulgence in baseless superstitions and illusions, a trait historically noted in communities resistant to Prophetic teachings. Such people exhibit a typical character of never acknowledging their own faults and wrongdoings. Instead of self-reflection and soul-searching, they always shift the blame of their self-inflicted troubles on others. For *Thamud*, the most convenient scapegoat was Hazrat Saleh and his followers due to their lacking in material wealth and power.

2. The verses 48 & 49 of Sura Naml (27) mentioned a group of nine influential men who belonged to the corridors of power and marked as the perpetrators and instigators of corruption (مفسدين) They were never interested in guiding their nation to the right path. In secrecy, they conspired and vowed to each other to fatally attack Hazrat Saleh and his family under the cover of night. Their evil scheme was not limited to killing the Prophet. Their wicked plot extended beyond the murder of the Prophet; they intended to feign innocence the next day before the heirs and broader kin of Hazrat Saleh. A complete and well-orchestrated plan of deceit.

3. In verse 49, mentioning of those planning to kill Hazrat Saleh as swearing by Allah is very meaningful. It raises an intriguing question about their faith. Does it imply that this group was among the believers who were hired for this sinister purpose? If true, this scenario is not unique but echoes throughout Prophetic history. The unexpected outcome of this scheming; culminating in the safety of Hazrat Saleh and ruination of those planning to harm him unknowingly, is enlightening. It serves as a reminder, as conveyed in verse 50, that against every evil scheme and malignant intention,

Allah has His plans, and the planning of Allah can never be thwarted.

4. Verses 12 and 14 of Sura Shams (91) in combination present another profound lesson. In the former verse the intent and willingness to kill the miracle of Allah is attributed to a single person while in the later verse, accountability for the act of denying the Prophet's advice and killing the camel encompassed all those who refused to accept *Iman* and stayed away from the *dawah* of Hazrat Saleh. This is a stark reminder of the fact that in the system of Allah, complicity and passive support for criminal acts aligns individuals with the perpetrator, making them equally punishable. In terms of Quranic teachings, this principle underscores the importance and key role of *Wilayat* and *Imamat* in human life. You may refer to verse 71 of Sura Isra (17). We must realize that *Wilayat* is universal and affects every domain and aspect of human life. It is pivotal in Godly systems as well as evil networks operating under the umbrella of *shaytan*.

5. No one was spared in *Thamud*, neither powerful nor weak. It did not matter whether people were supporting the act of killing the camel or not. Silent majority was also included in the ultimate *Azab*.

4.3. IMPORTANCE OF CORE GROUPS IN EVOLUTION OR DESTRUCTION OF A NATION

It is unambiguously observed that while describing the events of Hazrat Saleh, each Quranic narrative mentions a small group spearheading the aggression against him and the miracle he brought forth. Ultimately among them, a single individual, most vile and wicked, found the abominable guts to stretch his evil hands towards the miraculous sign of Allah, inflicting a fatal wound upon her. Consequently, the whole nation of *Thamud* met their doom and obliterated as enunciated in this verse of **Sura Qamar (54):**

V. 31: Indeed, We sent upon them a single 'mighty' blast [exceedingly loud thunderous sound], leaving them like the trampled twigs of fence-builders.

The focus on a group of nine persons, as we find in Sura Naml (27), and one exceedingly wicked man mentioned in Sura Shams (91), illustrates how the tyranny exhibited by the nation of *Thamud* was concentrated within a particular faction. In the *Ahadith* of *Masoomeen* (a.s) it is also mentioned that majority in the nation of *Thamud* were not active enemies of Hazrat Saleh but rather played the role of a silent majority. This suggests that while the active perpetrators were few, the broader community's passive stance decisively contributed to the causes that eventually led to their destruction and obliteration.

This elite group's ability to manipulate and control the masses underscores a significant social dynamic; the sway of a few individuals or a faction within a society can profoundly impact the collective behaviour and fate of the entire community. In the case of *Thamud*, Quran has illustrated the failure of people to critically evaluate the actions and directions of this powerful minority. Instead of questioning or opposing the misleading guidance of the elite, the community followed them blindly, contributing to an environment ripe for collective disobedience and rebellion against divine commands.

This highlights that in the life cycle of nations, their ultimate fate, whether it's ruination or prosperity, can crucially hinge on the presence of a core group. This group comprising merely 1-2% of the total population yet fully dedicated to the objectives they want, is sufficient to influence the nation's destiny. It is not necessary for every individual within the nation to exhibit same level of virtue or malice. Does it imply that the wider population have no role to play in destiny of nation? Certainly No! On the contrary, general masses have a pivotal role, though that contribution is mostly related to their endorsement and passive acceptance to the core group's actions and decisions. If a substantial number of people choose to rebel and adopt a different path, the intentions of that elite are blunted, and the nation may embark on an entirely different course. The Quranic narratives detailing the struggles of Bani Israel against *Firon* and the Muslims against the tyrants of Mecca, exemplify how collective dissent of common and oppressed people, under the guidance of an honest and truthful leadership, can overturn the influence of the dominant elite and steer a nation towards liberation from tyranny and oppression.

Before concluding this section and the chapter, I would like to present two examples from Quran that elucidate the influence of an elite group on the destiny of nations; although in a positive sense. Towards the end of Sura Tawba (9) there is a verse where Allah encourages a group among *momineen* to leave their homes, and journey to distant places where they could find the divine teachers. The wayfarers must spend sufficient time in their presence to be trained in Godly values. The verse reads:

Sura Tawba (9)

V. 122: And it is not (obligatory) for the *momineen* to go forth [leave their homes] all at once. Why not a party from every group come forward to [seek knowledge and] gain in-depth understanding of the religion (دين), and to warn their (respective) people after returning to them, so that they (the entire nation) may be cautious (of the consequences of traversing the wrong path).

It is worth noting that the awakening and spiritual evolution of an entire nation from ignorance, as well as their vigilance in preparing for the *Akherat* is dependent on the group that possesses in-depth knowledge of *Deen*. That elite group we know as *Mujtahed* has been assigned the responsibility of warning the people and making them aware of divine retributions in case of negligence and carelessness towards the teachings of Prophet.

The battle of trench (غزوه خندق), which took place in fifth year A.H., is another example highlighting the importance of a core group. Quran has described the state and condition of Muslims during the siege, living in Medina, in a unique manner. According to verses in **Sura Ahzab (33),** the Muslims were divided into at least five groups when they found themselves surrounded by an infidel army of ten thousand soldiers. At that juncture, Muslims lacked the strength and numbers for combat, nor was there any escape route available to them. The atmosphere gradually turned into one of gloom and disappointment. Only the help of Allah (نصرت الهی) could offer protection and deliverance, but the divine help does not come for nothing. It demands the *momineen* or Muslims to be at a certain level of *bandagi* and *Iman*. Alarmingly, verses describe majority of Muslims to be either grappling with spiritual ailments like love of Dunya and hypocrisy, or they were faltering in their resolve and courage to endure these harsh trials. Amidst this chaos, Allah mentions one group within the Muslims who were in fact, rejoicing the apparently despairing circumstances and yearning to lay their lives for meeting the Beloved (ذات حق تعالیٰ). Their presence triggered the divine mercy to act leading to a miraculous change in fortunes, forcing the *kafer* army to retreat and lifting their siege of Medina.

V.22: And when the momineen saw the (enemy) alliance, they said, "This is what Allah and His Rasool had promised us." And (this event) only increases them in *Iman* and submission.

V.23: Among the momineen there are men who have proven the truth of what they promised. Some of them have fulfilled their pledge (by giving their lives) while other are waiting their turn.

CHAPTER 5
CONCLUDING REMARKS

We have now concluded the analytical study of the lives of three Prophets who lived before Hazrat Ibrahim. Throughout this exploration, we discovered a more or less set pattern of opposition encountered by these early Prophets, which was met with a similar kind of response from Allah, a devastating *Azab*. These events have helped us in clearly comprehending the factors and reasons that trigger the advent of *Azab* and culminate in destruction of a nation. We also learnt the critical lesson that material wealth and prosperity offer no protection from ruination when people persist in their refusal to accept Allah's message.

Along the course of study, numerous lessons and topics of *Marefat* emerged, some of which were illustrated and discussed while many of them still remain unexplored. However, the main expectation is that the readers are learning and grasping the approach to combine, integrate, and delve deeper into the meanings of Quranic verses. For many, the manner in which the discussions are developed might be novel and encountered for the first time. Yet, persevering with this methodology can unveil a fundamental truth about divine revelation: Quran does not tell stories but enrich and educate us with life building principles through references to the past events. The lives of Prophets of Allah are like minarets and beacons, illuminating the path of human endeavour towards their ultimate fate, unimpeded by the barriers of time and space.

With Allah's permission, our next book in the series on Prophets and Prophethood will be on the Quranic study of the life of Hazrat Ibrahim. That great Prophet is the patriarch of all Prophets who came after him and mentioned as the father of Muslim Ummah in the last verse of Sura Hajj. The reverence with which he is mentioned in Quran fills us with awe and immense respect.

I earnestly hope and pray that this effort finds acceptance in the Presence of my *Rab* and my Imam and blossoms into a garden of *Marefat* whose fragrance benefits me and my dear friends who have accompanied me on this journey of enlightening their souls with the *Noor* of Quran and *Masoomeen* (a.s).

We conclude with prayers for prosperity, wellbeing, safety and unity for all momin men and women, living in every country and city in this world. We pray for the Maghferat or every *momin* and *momina* and earliest possible coming of Imam e Asr (a.s).

آخر دعوانا ان الحمد لله ربّ العالمين

9 781763 572508